TALES OF A
Shirtmaker

A JEWISH UPBRINGING
IN NORTH CAROLINA

ALSO BY SUSAN TAYLOR BLOCK
The Wrights of Wilmington
Wilmington's Confederate General: William MacRae
Dressed in Sunlight: Eleanor Wright Beane (with Eleanor Wright Beane)

PUBLISHED BY THE BOYS AND GIRLS BRIGADE, INC.
The Character Factory: A History of the Boys' Brigade

PUBLISHED BY THE CAPE FEAR MUSEUM
Along the Cape Fear
Cape Fear Lost
Cape Fear Beaches

PUBLISHED BY THE LOWER CAPE FEAR HISTORICAL SOCIETY
AND THE NEW HANOVER COUNTY PUBLIC LIBRARY
Wilmington Through the Lens of Louis T. Moore
Van Eeden

PUBLISHED BY AIRLIE FOUNDATION, INC.
Airlie: The Garden of Wilmington

PUBLISHED BY CAPE FEAR GARDEN CLUB
Belles and Blooms: Cape Fear Garden Club and the N.C. Azalea Festival

PUBLISHED BY ST. JAMES CHURCH
Temple of Our Fathers: St. James Church (1729–2004)

To John and Sandy — merry Christmas! STB

From — Rick & Rose

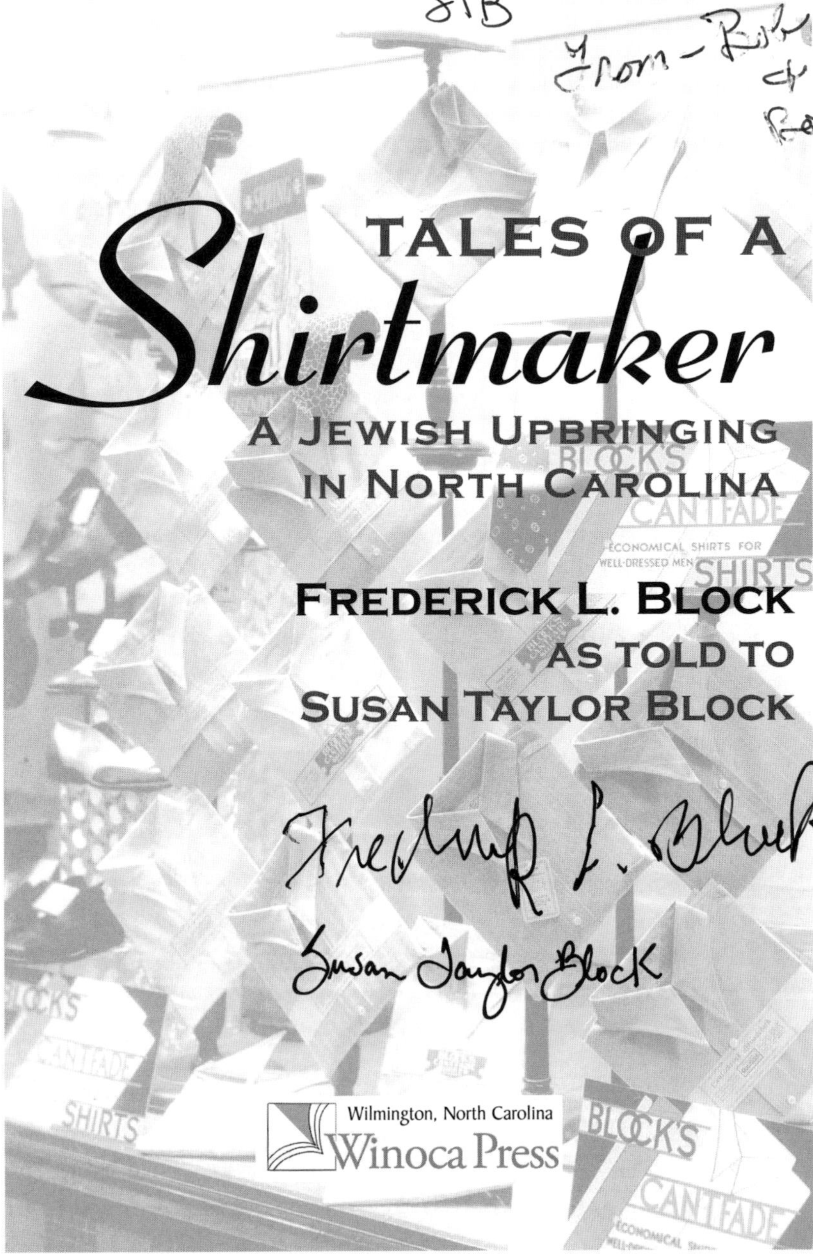

TALES OF A
Shirtmaker

A JEWISH UPBRINGING IN NORTH CAROLINA

FREDERICK L. BLOCK

AS TOLD TO
SUSAN TAYLOR BLOCK

Frederick L. Block

Susan Taylor Block

Wilmington, North Carolina
Winoca Press

Tales of a Shirtmaker: A Jewish Upbringing in North Carolina
© Copyright 2005 by Susan Taylor Block

Published by Winoca Press
106 North 16th Street, Wilmington, NC 28401-3819 USA
www.winocapress.com
Available from the publisher or from the authors:
P. O. Box 3691, Wilmington, NC 28406   USA / bookmart@ec.rr.com

Printed in the United States of America
07 06 05   5 4 3 2 1

Library of Congress Cataloging-in-Publication Data
Block, Frederick L., 1927—
Tales of a shirtmaker: a Jewish upbringing in North Carolina / Frederick L. Block
as told to Susan Taylor Block.
p. cm.
Includes bibliographical references.
ISBN 0-9755910-1-0
Block, Frederick L., 1927—   2. Block Shirts (Firm) 3. Jews—North Carolina—
Wilmington—Biography.   4. Wilmington (N.C.)—Biography.   I. Block, Susan
Taylor, 1951—   II. Title.
F265.J5B55 2005
975.6'27004924'092—dc22   2004031065

*The author is grateful to Beverly Tetterton at the New Hanover County Public Library,
Eli Naeher at the Lower Cape Fear Historical Society, and Tim Bottoms at the Cape Fear
Museum for special care in providing some of the photos. Barbara Brannon has done
exceptional work as advisor, editor, and book designer. Betty H. and Joseph W. Taylor, Jr.,
along with John Burney, Jr., David Block, Nathan Schwartz, Joe Sheppard, Sandra
Stadiem and Sonny Simpson, and Michael Whaley, provided additional information.*

*On the cover: A young Fred Block and men of the Block family at the Scotts Hill farm,
about 1939; model window display for Block's Cantfade Shirts line; Sadie Stadiem Block
and sons Fred (left) and David, 1936. The striped oxford cloth pattern in the background
is taken from a Block's fabric sample book, circa 1965. These and other photographs are
from the collection of the author, except where noted.*

This book is dedicated to the memory of William Block (1877–1954), quietly devout and perennially kind

CONTENTS

List of Illustrations   *ix*
Genealogy: The Block Family of Wilmington   *xii*
Introduction: A Little Background   *Susan Taylor Block*   *xv*
   Nathan Block and the Block Shirt Factory of Wilmington   *1*
   Little Boy Block   *4*
   School Days   *7*
   Union Station to Grand Central   *15*
   Kinston and the Stadiems   *17*
   Flown from the Coop   *25*
   Traffic Boy Block   *28*
   Life in a Streetcar City   *30*
   Set Apart   *35*
   Ma Sadie and Freddie Boy   *43*
   Sports in the 1930s   *46*
   Food Customs in the Block Household   *50*
   Summers at Carolina Beach   *55*
   Moving   *65*
   Shirt Tales   *71*
   Dark Clouds   *79*
   Tales Told out of School   *82*
   Different Days   *87*
   Duty!   *91*
   A Block in Blue Heaven   *95*
   Georgia Frolic   *99*
   Four-Wheel School   *104*
   More Duty   *111*
   Back to Work   *117*
   Southland   *124*
   Watching the Pennies   *132*
   Spreading Out   *135*
   New Yawk   *147*
   Today   *150*
Notes   *155*

ILLUSTRATIONS

Nathan Block, about 1905   *xvii*

Fannie Block with sons Charles and Nathan, about 1904   *xviii*

Charles and Nathan Block in Baltimore, about 1913   *xix*

Fannie Herman Block, seller of real estate options, about 1922   *xx*

Block Shirts and Nehi drinks at 702 North Front Street in
      mid-1920s   *xxi*

Hyman and Yetta Shapiro Stadiem, with children, about 1912   *xxii*

Sadie Stadiem as Little Red Riding Hood for a community play   *xxii*

Betty Serrins Stadiem of Greensboro, about 1895   *xxii*

H. Stadiem logo   *xxiii*

Block's Cantfade Shirts logo   *xxiv*

Greenfield Street wing of Block Shirts, the firm's cutting
      department   *xxiv*

Interior of Southland's Hanover Street factory, about 1926   *xxv*

William Block, about 1945   *xxvi*

Nathan Block, about 1949   *xxvi*

Fred Block, about 1984   *xxvii*

Siblings Barbara Block Austin, Lynda Block Bohbot, Alison Block Getz,
      and Billy Block, 2004   *xxviii*

Susan and Fred Block, at home, 1995   *xxix*

Southland Manufacturing order form   *xxx*

Greenfield Street factory, 1937   *3*

A young Fred Block on family vacation in Florida   *5*

Fred Block and grandfather William Block, about 1928   *6*

Fred Block atop one of Jack Farrar's horses, about 1937   *6*

Howard-Graham Kindergarten certificate   *7*

Fred Block, age fifteen months, in front of the Nathan Shane house,
      Chestnut Street   *8*

1932 production by St. James Church Kindergarten   *9*

L. W. Fonvielle and Fred Block, about 1936   *11*

Isaac Bear School, about 1933   *13*

Longley lawn at 111 North 15th Street   *14*

H. E. Longley and son Henry, about 1938   *14*

Siblings Moses and Sadie Stadiem, about 1908   *17*

Isaac Stadiem   *19*

Siblings David Stadiem and Sadie Stadiem Block, 1998   *21*

Fred and Nathan Block on the Stadiems' front porch,
     Kinston, 1942   *22*

Fred, Sadie, and David Block on the side porch on Chestnut
     Street, 1936   *24*

Temple of Israel, 1 South Front Street   *36*

The old synagogue, 313 Walnut Street   *37*

B'nai Israel synagogue today   *42*

Sir William Shirts logo   *44*

Aerial view of the Block Shirt factory, about 1938   *45*

Advertisement for Block shirts   *45*

Baseball board in front of the Murchison Building, 1930s   *47*

Fred and David Block, about 1938   *49*

Claude Howell depictions of Wilmington City Market   *52*

Nathan and Sadie Block at the "Please Don't Rain House" on
     Carolina Beach, about 1934   *56*

Miriam Stadiem, about 1933   *58*

Fred Block at Carolina Beach, about 1937   *59*

The fishermen of Seabreeze   *61*

Fred, Sadie, David, and Nathan Block at 711 Forest Hills Drive,
     about 1941   *67*

Fred Block at 711 Forest Hills Drive, 1941   *68*

Bill for construction on the Blocks' Forest Hills home, 1940   *69*

Nathan E. Block in the South Third Street factory, about 1951   *73*

Sadie Block and two servicemen, Forest Hills   *74*

Ann Wolf and Fred Loeb, about 1941, as pictured in Van Eeden   *75*

Fred and Ann Wolf Loeb of Silver Spring, Maryland, 1990s   *75*

David and Fred Block, photographed by holocaust escapee
     Fred Wolff in 1939   *77*

Fred Block, Howard Guld, William Block, Nathan Block, and Joe Block,
     at Scotts Hill farm, about 1939   *80*

New Hanover High School, Market Street   *86*

Fred Block in his Citadel uniform   *92*

Father and son, Nathan and Fred Block, before a college
     football game   *96*

Fred Block's University of Georgia student ID photo and athletics
     ticket, 1946–47   *100*

Nathan Block in his office at Southland, 1952   *102*

℥ x ℥

Window display featuring the Cantfade label   *105*
Southland promotional card   *106*
Fred Block, Betty Lou Morrow, Ann Everett, and John Burney,
    about 1945   *108*
The Cantfade Christmas party, about 1948   *109*
The *Cantfade* in the Inland Waterway, about 1949   *110*
Sinking of the *Maipu*   *112*
Certificate from the *General Hersey*   *112*
Fred Block on leave, French Riviera, 1952   *113*
Fred Block and two soldier friends, Forest Hills, 1951   *114*
Fred's new office at the plant   *119*
Joe Block and his date, Irene, New York City, 1954   *122*
Southland factory workers line up for Fourth of July party, 1966   *125*
Longtime presser Lucille Tyson and other Block workers, 1966   *125*
Block cutter Henry Croom, 1966   *126*
Nathan and Fred Block, about 1977   *128*
Modeling Block shirts: Carlisle Jenkins, Henry Nunalee, Kevin Dineen,
    and Billy Block   *129*
Nathan and Fred Block at Wrighstville Beach Marina, about 1971   *130*
Board members of the North Carolina National Bank   *133*
Cutting tables at the Block factory   *134*
Trailer used to transport goods between Wilmington and Benson   *137*
Mildred Rackley, manager of the Benson plant, 1966   *139*
Bob George, manager of the Newport factory, 1966   *139*
Sadie Block with son Fred, 1981   *143*
Trade delegation departs for China, 1970s   *144*
Fred Block's return from an overseas business trip, 1979   *144*
Trade mission attorney Martin Klingenberg and Fred Block at the
    Great Wall of China, 1979   *145*
Block business card, New York office   *148*
Longtime Block employees Joe Maultsby and Alton Ketchum, with
    Nathan Block at the new factory, about 1981   *149*
Greenfield Street wing of Block Shirts   *152*
Block employees Magdalene Johnson, Doris Ashe, Holly Long,
    and Brad Murray, about 1984   *153*
Fred Block at Figure Eight Island, about 1992   *154*

THE BLOCK FAMILY
OF WILMINGTON

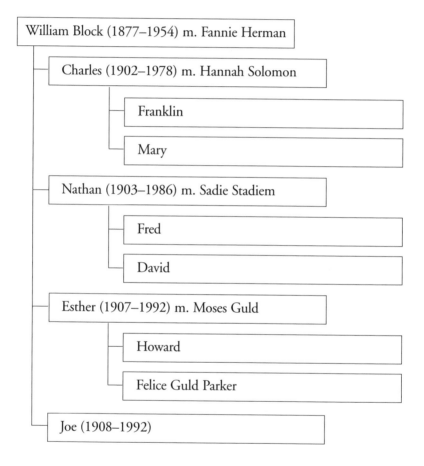

William Block (1877–1954) m. Fannie Herman

  Charles (1902–1978) m. Hannah Solomon

    Franklin

    Mary

  Nathan (1903–1986) m. Sadie Stadiem

    Fred

    David

  Esther (1907–1992) m. Moses Guld

    Howard

    Felice Guld Parker

  Joe (1908–1992)

TALES OF A *Shirtmaker*

A JEWISH UPBRINGING
IN NORTH CAROLINA

A Little Background

Susan Taylor Block

It is a myth, explains Theodore Rosengarten in his introduction to *A Portion of the People: Three Hundred Years of Southern Jewish Life,* that there were no Jews in the South. Rather, writes Eli N. Evans in the preface to the volume, the American South had welcomed Jews as far back as the seventeenth century, and the Carolinas in particular had been

> a fantasy come true . . . a place of dreams where Jews could live free in a kind of promised land, free to worship as they saw fit, free to practice any profession, free to trade and to make partnerships with gentiles, free to vote, free to own property and will it to their heirs. (xv)

Whether William Block, grandfather of Frederick Lee Block, consciously held such a view is not known. But the son of Eastern European immigrants must have seen opportunity and advantage in North Carolina in the early years of the twentieth century, when he moved to Wilmington from Baltimore and founded an apparel business that would sustain his family for years to come.

Fred Block has held a place of transition in this family and its enterprises. As a child in the port city of Wilmington, North Carolina, he enjoyed the comforts of a supporting, peaceful community, a loving extended family, and middle-class privilege. As a young man he served in the military, experienced university life, and learned his father's business from the ground up. He also learned about difference, taking note of the way the world was changing after World War II. He went on to lead the Block firm through shifts in management philosophy during a time when apparel manufacturing was just beginning to move to overseas production.

It is Fred Block's stories that I relate here, only minimally edited from the way he first told them to me. Taken together they form a picture of Wilmington from just after World War I, through the tumult of the second World War, and on into the era of civil rights and integration. They are episodes rather than a chronicle; there is no attempt to be comprehensive, or to show life from any other perspective. But they preserve a glimpse of a particular time and place that even now is gone—and for that I am glad to play a part in recording them.

William Block, Fred Block's grandfather, was the son of Moses and Rachel (Rebecca)[1] Fain Block, who lived in that area of Europe between the Baltic and Black Seas known in the 1800s as the Pale of Settlement and now known as Latvia. William, one of eleven children, was born in the city of Riga on December 22, 1877. Moses Block's family had originally lived in Germany but moved to Latvia to escape persecution. Rachel's family operated a shipbuilding business in Riga, but her husband chose the path of many of his ancestors in Germany and became a rabbi and a professor of theology. The only physical description of Moses that has survived regards his exceptional height, a trait he shared with all his sons except William. He died when William was a child, leaving his large family so poor that some of them had to sleep on the floor.

William's mother, Rebecca Block, was busy with a shirtmaking business that she ran successfully until her death at age 85. Perhaps this is why a New York newspaper once stated that William Block "might well be said to have been born in a shirt box."[2] In 1890, when William was only thirteen, his mother sent him abroad to Baltimore, where he became a peddler to earn money for his sister's dowry or "dob."

William Block was close to, and possibly distantly related to, a community of Jews from Riga who lived in and around Baltimore, Maryland, whose surnames included Herman, Millison, and Weiner. The Millison family name was originally Levine—but the first member to reach Baltimore bought a peddler business from a man named Millison. Wishing to save money, he forewent a new license and simply became "Mr. Millison."

Most of the Herman family worked outside Baltimore in a crossroads community called Hermanville, where they owned a store and ran the post office. "I remember visiting there," said Fred Millison, a descendant of the family, in 1992. "Business was slow at one time and they were advised to stock up on reading glasses so that their aging customers could read their Bibles. They bought them from a Mr. Epstein in Baltimore for fifty cents a pair and sold them for two dollars. Business picked up for a while."

Nathan Block, about 1905 (photo by the Kirkness Studio, Baltimore)

By 1900, William Block had married Fannie Leah Herman, the daughter of Charles and Sarah Herman. The newlyweds lived next door to the bride's brother and sister-in-law, Philip and Callie Herman. Philip was the postmaster for whom Hermanville was named in 1898. In addition to Fannie's daughter, Yetta, from a previous marriage, Fannie Herman and William Block had four children: Charles Morris Block (b. 1902), Nathan Ellis Block (b. 1903), Esther Block (b. 1907), and Joseph

Fannie Block poses with sons Charles (left) and Nathan (center) in this studio photo, about 1904.

Manfred Block (b. 1908).

By 1918 William Block had become a partner in a factory making undergarments and had moved his family to Baltimore's fashionable Eutaw Place. Fannie, a businessperson in her own right, bought and sold real estate options. Yetta, the eldest child, died February 23, 1923, at the age of 27, leaving a seven-year-old daughter, Shirley. Because the child's father was not in a position to raise her, William and Fannie Block adopted her.

In an effort to expand the company, William Block's son Nathan moved to Wilmington, North Carolina, in 1923 to start a new factory. He had made his very first visit there the year before, after one of their Baltimore salesmen recommended the city for its beauty and the presence of two cotton mills, Bellwill and Spofford. Nathan brought along twenty-five weathered sewing machines but was undaunted at the prospect of starting with so little. Nathan was able to do virtually every chore that was called for in a factory, including machine repair. The local paper took note: "Machinery for the equipment of the Block Manufacturing Company, a Baltimore concern which is to set up an underwear plant at Front and Hanover streets, is expected to reach the city today. Nathan Block, of the firm, will arrive shortly in the capacity of local manager for the main home plant, which will continue to operate in Baltimore."[3]

Very soon, William and the entire Block family moved south to Wilmington. Eventually, all three of William's sons—Charles, Nathan, and Joe—worked with him. William Block bought a house at 3 South Fourth Street, next to the Temple of Israel, and his three sons continued to live with their father, as they had previously done in Baltimore.

The first small, temporary factory was located near Eighth and Castle Streets. But soon the Blocks leased a bigger space on Hanover Street from Solomon Bear, the building previously housing the E. L. Mathews Candy Company. The Hanover Street factory was heated by pot-bellied stoves. Underwear sewn by the Block factory, often made in suits of matching shirts and boxer shorts, was shipped from Wilmington to longstanding customers in Baltimore, New Mexi-

Charles (left) and Nathan Block in Baltimore, about 1913

co, Kansas, Boston, Philadelphia, and Savannah. Soon after switching from underwear to making dress shirts, the new firm, Southland Manufacturing Company, was turning out 4,800 shirts a week.[4]

William Block's wife, Fannie Leah Herman Block, had already been in declining health for five years when the family moved to Wilmington. She was under the steady care of Dr. J. B. Cranmer, a neighbor who lived at 311 Market Street. Dr. Cranmer examined her for the last time on February 11, 1924; the following day, when only forty-five years old, she died at home of "bronchial and cardiac asthma." Fannie was buried in

Baltimore the following afternoon, in the Herring Run
Hebrew Cemetery, next to her
daughter, Yetta Lasky. Their
graves are in the Beth Yehuda
Anshe Kurland section, a part of
the cemetery where many inter-
related families from Riga are
buried. Three of Fannie's grandchildren would be named for her,
sharing her initials "F. L.": Frederick Lee Block, Franklin Lee
Block, and Felice Leah Guld.

Soon after the death of his
wife, William Block sold the
home he had purchased on
Fourth Street to put more capital
in the business. He then rented a
house from his friend, Willie
Rosenmann, at 14 South Fifth
Street. There, the whole family

*Fannie Herman Block, seller of real estate
options, in Baltimore, about 1922 (photo
by the Kirkness Studio, Baltimore)*

became well acquainted with their neighbor Champ Davis, who would
eventually become president of the Atlantic Coast Line Railroad.

A fire in the fall of 1927 destroyed the factory, but soon sewing
machines were humming again in the same rebuilt location. In 1930,
Block or "Southland" purchased the Sol Bear Winery building in the
1100 block of South Front Street as a rental property and a backup space
for the factory. It was leased for many years to Farrar Moving and Storage. In 1935, Southland began operating from a building on Greenfield
Street that had formerly housed the Wilmington Printing Company.
They later expanded the plant to include a wing on South Third Street.
The Greenfield Street portion of the "new" factory then became the
firm's cutting department.

In 1926, Nathan Block married Sadie Stadiem of Kinston, North Carolina. Sadie's family originated in Prussia, where their surname had been both Staviscofsky and Scheindam before it was merged to Stadiem, perhaps by an immigration clerk. The rabbi who married Nathan and Sadie Block was concerned about the differences in Nathan's German Orthodox Jewish background and Sadie's Eastern European Jewish roots, and he advised the couple to work hard at staying close. It must have worked: their marriage would last until Nathan's death in 1986.

Sadie's father, Hyman Stadiem (1882–1937), was revered in the farming community of Kinston, where he founded the H. Stadiem clothing store in 1903. Hyman had learned the retail business from his father, David, who had established a clothing store in Greensboro. David's son Abe remained in Greensboro to mind the family store while another son, Lewis, started a new one in Durham. Hyman chose Kin-

Block Shirts and Nehi drinks, strange bedfellows, shared a building at 702 North Front Street in the mid-1920s. The structure housed Sol Bear and Company Winery until Prohibition took effect. There was a fourth floor before the fire of October 1927. (Courtesy of Cape Fear Museum)

Hyman and Yetta Shapiro Stadiem of Kinston, North Carolina, about 1912, with children (from left) Jacob, Moses, Isaac, Sadie, and Abraham. Sadie would marry Nathan Block of Wilmington in 1926.

Sadie Stadiem (Block) was two years old in 1908, when she dressed as Little Red Riding Hood for a community play.

Sadie's grandmother, Betty Serrins Stadiem of Greensboro, North Carolina, about 1895

ston because "it was a good place." When Hyman Stadiem died suddenly at the age of 55, the local paper ran an editorial that exclaimed:

> Thousands came to know him. None found fault with him. His was an honorable life, a religious life. They say his benevolences were numerous and unrevealed.
>
> His home life was as perfect as any. The family became 10, and the affection that ruled in the household at Gordon and Independence streets was the finest thing in the neighborhood.
>
> Death did Hyman Stadiem no harm. It gathered him to his fathers, and they dwell in happiness.[5]

The Kinston store celebrated a century of business in 2003 and continues to operate. Hyman Stadiem, great-grandson of immigrant David Stadiem and grandson of the first Hyman, owns the store today. His

father, David, age 87, still waits attentively on customers several days a week.

Eventually William Block remarried, to Lena Wolk of Wilmington.[6] The Block families occupied several addresses in the Carolina Heights and Winoca Terrace neighborhoods. Lena had built two homes in Carolina Heights: one at 1618 Princess Street, and a "twin" house, positioned sideways on its lot, that still stands at 204 North 15th Street. William and Lena Block lived at 1618 Princess Street from at least 1930 until 1935. When their marriage failed, William went to live for a year with his son Nathan at 1404 Chestnut Street. About 1935, William purchased 1618 Princess Street from his former wife, and returned there along with his extended family: his youngest son, Joe, his daughter, Esther Block Guld, her husband, Moe, and their two children, Howard and Felice.

Block Shirts, or Southland Manufacturing Corporation, went on to be a major national manufacturing concern and grew to include multi-

ple factories in the United States. Their products were sold under the labels Sir William, Freddie Boy, Southland, and Block. The factory also made shirts for Belk department stores, which sold under the name Andhurst, as well as shirts for many other retailers, including Saks Fifth Avenue, Macy's, Gimbel's, Broadway, and Hudson's.

The Greenfield Street wing of Block Shirts (once home to Wilmington Printing) became the factory's cutting department.

In 1937, Southland Manufacturing Company was the largest shirt company in the South. By 1937 Southland was making 24,000 shirts each week and employing 350 workers. The company's success fed other successes. Over half the cloth used at Southland was actually woven in the South. Cotton farmers and textile workers benefited: sixteen bales of

The interior of Southland's Hanover Street factory, about 1926

cotton translated into 33,000 yards of fabric that, in turn, became 1,175 shirts.

Southland employed fourteen traveling salesmen in 1937 and sold their shirts in 1,500 retail outlets in the United States, the West Indies, and Canada. "Ninety-eight per cent of the Block workers are Wilmington residents," reported the *Wilmington Morning Star* for February 14, 1937, "and many have become highly skilled through their years of work with the concern, finding invaluable training and employment simultaneously."

William Block died of pneumonia on August 8, 1954, and was buried at B'Nai Israel Cemetery in Wilmington. After William Block's death, sons Nathan, Charles, and Joe Block continued to work for the company. Fred's younger brother, David Block, Charles's son, Franklin Block, and Esther Guld's husband, Moe, and son Howard also joined the

William Block, about 1945

family business.

When Nathan Block retired in 1969, Fred Block was named president of Block Shirts. In addition to leading the firm, Fred went on to serve as a founder of the Cape Fear Academy in Wilmington, a director of the Bank of North Carolina, and a president of the Figure Eight Island board of directors.

By 1972 family tensions and changing conditions in the industry led to a merger of Block Industries, Inc., and National Service Industries, Inc. Fred arranged the sale and continued as president and CEO until 1985. He oversaw the building of the shipping department on Burnett Boulevard in Wilmington as well as new shirt factories in the islands, in Arizona, and in Benson, Newport, and Rowland, North Carolina. He also built the College Road Block Industries building in Wilmington, in 1980. He eventually made fifty trips to the Far East, making new arrangements for shirt manufacturing that would improve business, but that would also bring sadness when the Block sewing rooms became obsolete.

Nonetheless the Block Shirt business continued to grow as long as Block family members were at the helm. In 1985, Fred Block resigned when he was accused of mismanagement, a charge from which he was exonerated in federal court. When Fred Block left the firm, the company

Nathan Block, about 1949

Fred Block, about 1984

was grossing $100 million a year, and Block shirts were carried in some 10,000 retail outlets nationwide.[7]

In 1992, National Service Industries sold Block Industries to a group of investors headed by former Bloomingdale's chairman Marvin Traub. Today an investor group led by Stewart Kim continues to run Block with offices in New York and Alabama.

Nathan Block, who originally brought the Block shirtmaking enterprise to Wilmington, died in 1986. Sadie Block died in 2000, at the age of ninety-four.

Charles Block, eldest of William Block's three sons, died in 1978. He is survived by his wife, Hannah, who became a Wilmington icon. In her nineties she is still a voice in Wilmington politics and many organizations. An honorary Green Beret, she is a former mayor pro tem, a former city councilwoman, and a former beauty queen coach whose most famous trainee was Maria Fletcher, Miss America 1962.

Charles and Hannah's son, Franklin Block, graduated from the Citadel in 1959 and Wake Forest Law School in 1976. He served as U.S. magistrate, built a successful private practice, and served in the North

Carolina Senate. Franklin and his wife, Wendy Barshay Block, are involved in many charities and cultural organizations in Wilmington.

Esther and Moe Guld's son, Howard, resigned when Block was sold, in 1972.

In 1954, Fred Block married Geraldine (Jeri) Susan Fox (1935–1987). They had four children: William Bentley Block (b. 1956; married to Audra Wetherill), Alison Henri Block (b. 1957; married to Donald Getz), Lynda Leigh Block (b. 1960; married to Meir Bohbot), and Barbara Ann Block (b. 1964; married to William Austin).

In 1991 Fred Block married Elizabeth Susan Taylor—the compiler of this volume and others, with Fred's encouragement and help. Since 1990, his family has grown to include two stepdaughters, Taylor Cromartie and Catherine Gerdes, and four grandchildren, Nathan Oliver-Block, Elijah Austin, Jacob Austin, and Joshua Austin.

Since his retirement, Fred Block has developed a decided aversion to dress shirts and ties. With his wife and stepdaughter Catherine, he lives

Siblings Barbara Block Austin, Lynda Block Bohbot, Alison Block Getz, and Billy Block, in 2004

Susan and Fred Block, at home, 1995

a quiet life in his hometown. Fred continues to amuse and charm those who love him. Speaking in the fast-disappearing old accent of coastal Carolina, he tells his stories whenever they are requested. Though sometimes they include more details than at others, his tales are always the same. And there are no exaggerations. No bragging.

Former employees still speak to him in restaurants and stores and offices. "Hey, Mr. Freddie!" they call out. And he still, when confronted with a brand new shirt, will patiently study every feature. In the collar, stitches, buttonholes, and seams, he sees a world known to but a dwindling few.

———

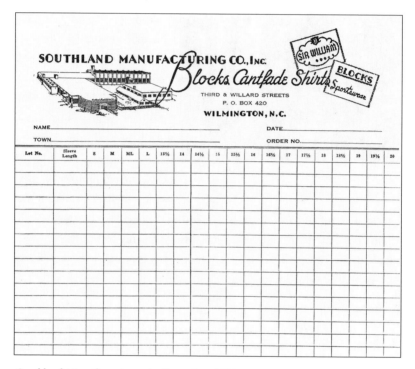

Southland Manufacturing order form, circa 1959

NATHAN BLOCK AND THE BLOCK SHIRT FACTORY OF WILMINGTON

By 1991, Fred Block was in his early 60s and, with encouragement, had grown fond of reminiscing. These are his stories.

My father, Nathan Block, moved from Baltimore to Wilmington in 1923 to start a shirt factory. He brought twenty-five used sewing machines with him. In those times, as in the Far East today, the wages for factory labor were much lower in the South than in established industrial areas. In 1923, there was no minimum wage law in the United States. They just had local wages. The old North sort of migrated south. Factories in Boston and other places closed up.

Boston, they used to tell me, was like the Orient of the 1980s, when I first traveled there. Factory owners would give young girls from all the small towns room and board and let them stay there as long as they worked in the factory. The girls would go home every other weekend. They would have Sunday off and they would go home and visit their family. And that's exactly what they did in Taiwan, Hong Kong, and Korea in the 1980s. They would go to school there, eat there, sleep there—from the time they were fifteen years old. It was a sort of trade school apprenticeship situation. At Block, we kept to the rules, and our workers were not that young.

Wilmington was a small city, and my father liked it here and in 1926 he married my mother, who was from another small North Carolina town. I was born November 17, 1927. My parents stayed here and raised their sons and had a lot of good years in the shirt business.

When my father arrived in Wilmington he came all by himself. He found the place on a prior trip, and when he got here with the machines, he started hiring people to make underwear. That's what they had made in Baltimore, at the Block-Lasky Factory. He ran the Wilmington plant for a while, trained operators, and saw that things were going well. That's when they decided to close the factory in Baltimore.

Not long before my father came here, there had been great sadness in Baltimore when my father's half-sister, Yetta, died. My grandmother had been married before, and Yetta was her only child by that marriage. My grandfather treated her as his own child and so she was the oldest child in the household. Yetta married a man from Baltimore, and they had a daughter named Shirley. Shirley was just a little girl when her mother died.

So then, my grandfather treated Shirley as if she were one of his own children. Her mother had been treated as the oldest, and Shirley was treated as the youngest even though neither was his child. So even though Shirley was my father's half-niece, she spoke of him as her brother. My grandmother did not live long after they moved to Wilmington. They said she died of a broken heart because of Yetta's death.

Soon after moving here, Daddy made a new friend, a salesman named Willie Rosenmann. Later on, my parents would rent from him. Willie lived at 12 South Fifth Street in Wilmington. My parents (Nathan and Sadie), Charlie, Joe, Esther, Shirley, and William Block all lived at 14 South Fifth Street in 1927. One day, Willie advised Pa to get out of underwear manufacturing and start making shirts. He told my father, "There's no money in underwear."

So Pa started making shirts. The change meant more than just a big jump in profit. It just seemed more respectable to make shirts. We could talk about shirts anywhere. But underwear? My father was smart. He could do anything in the factory, and he invented some new factory equipment. He knew finance and kept everything going right. He came up short on salesmanship, though. He was abrupt and very frank.

One of the first girls my father ever hired, in 1923, was a candid, very down-to-earth woman named Lily Mason. She turned into one of the best sewing supervisors we ever had. Funny thing was, she wouldn't hire any blondes. Most of the women who applied got their color from a bottle, but that didn't matter to Lily Mason. Wouldn't have any blondes. She was still working there in the 1940s.

Greenfield Street factory, 1937

LITTLE BOY BLOCK

Our little family left the house at 14 South Fifth Street about the time I was born. I think my mother got us out of there. She was in charge of things at our house, while my father was in charge of things at work. That was always the case. On Fifth Street, my mother had no control and they had no privacy.

The first house I remember was the one at 1404 Chestnut Street, in a neighborhood known as Winoca Terrace. As far as any of us knew, the chestnut tree in our back yard was the only one on the street. The house was plain and two-story and had been used as a small private school by the former owner, Catherine Whitehead.

The whole time I was growing up, I called my mother Mama and my father Daddy. I think that is what all my friends called their parents, too. Later I started calling my mother Ma Sadie. It fit. By the time she died, most people called her that. And Daddy turned into Pa.

I guess my first childhood memory could be a trip to Florida I took with my mother and her parents and her sister, Miriam. I was three. We stopped by St. Augustine on the way down and spent the night. I was afraid to ride the elevator in the hotel, so my grandfather Stadiem held me in his arms as we rode it—even though I hit him on the head. After that, I loved the elevator and I rode it up and down with the elevator operator.

Then we went to Miami and I don't remember much about that.

On the way back, we drove along the western coast and we bought some tomatoes near Tampa. We bought a bushel of green tomatoes. That was the only way they sold them.

To our surprise, the next day, we saw one turning red. And as they turned red, we started eating them—just like you eat an apple. We would drive along munching on tomatoes. I know I get my love of tomatoes from my mother. She loved tomatoes, pickles, pickled herring—and almost anything else that was pickled. Acidic foods.

My Stadiem grandparents, Hyman and Yetta, did not say

A young Fred Block on family vacation in Florida

much. My grandmother was a strong character. My mother told the story many times that the day I was born, she created a scene at Wilmington's James Walker Hospital. I was born at high noon. Ma Sadie said she heard the twelve o'clock whistle blow right as I was born. It was the middle of November, a time when tobacco selling cleared the streets of Kinston, North Carolina. The men in the family wouldn't have dreamed of leaving the store to go see a baby, so my grandmother was stranded. She didn't let it get her down. She just went out on the highway and flagged down a vehicle to take her to Wilmington. It happened to be a Salvation Army truck on its way here. They dropped her off at the hospital.

Yetta Stadiem went from room to room in the hospital looking for Ma Sadie. When she finally found the right room, a nurse came and stood in the doorway. "You can't come in here," she said to my four-

Above: Fred Block's grandfather William doted on his first grandson, shown here about 1928.

foot-nine grandmother. But Yetta just shoved that nurse right out of the doorway and pushed her way in to see her daughter and her first grandchild.

Another very early memory I have is of accidentally seeing a little girl in our neighborhood naked. It was the first time I had ever seen anything like that. I went straight home and told my mother that that little girl's mother was *very* mean.

"Why do you say that, Freddie?" she asked me. "Because her mother cut off her wee-wee," I answered.

Left: Fred Block atop one of Jack Farrar's horses, about 1937. Farrar kept his horses on a farm located at the southwest corner of College Road and Oleander Drive in Wilmington, which is today occupied by Alltel and Toys 'R' Us. Farrar leased the old Bear Winery at 1121 South Front Street from the Blocks and used it as a storage facility business for many years.

SCHOOL DAYS

When I was five, I went to kindergarten at St. James Church, the big Episcopal church on Market Street. That year they called it the Howard-Graham Kindergarten because the teachers were Louisa Howard and Mary Graham. My mother sent me there because it was considered the best kindergarten in town. I don't remember much about that, except my teacher. I couldn't say my g's then, so I called her Mrs. Dam. She was sweet to me, and I always had warm feelings for St. James Church because of her.

Growing up in Wilmington was fun for me. There was always something to do or something to see. My parents would take me to Echo Farms, down on Carolina Beach Road, to milk the cows, or on a ride to Wrightsville Beach or Carolina Beach. Sometimes we would go to Swart's Dairy in Castle Hayne. We went to Monkey Junction, where we would feed the monkeys. We would sometimes go to the little zoo at Greenfield Park, which was located on the west side of Third

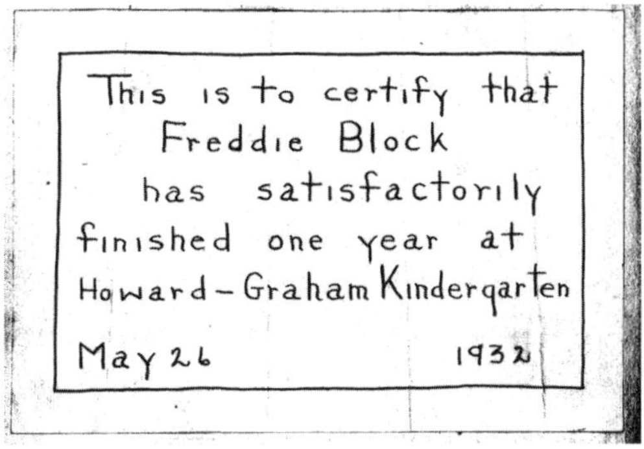

This is to certify that
Freddie Block
has satisfactorily
finished one year at
Howard-Graham Kindergarten
May 26   1932

Street and had a bear—a big black bear.

Sometimes we would drive out to a speakeasy. Pa enjoyed a drink. I remember the ten-gallon keg he kept under a step in the Chestnut Street house during Prohibition. He bought whisky at a place out on Market Street across from the Blue Top Lodge. I remember riding downtown one Sunday. We were going down Water Street and when we got to the Custom House, there were black men out there with axes chopping up cases of whisky and then destroying the bottles. I remember my father saying, "That's awful. How could anybody do something like that?"

Pa also said, "I bet somebody's under the dock"—collecting the spillage!

When I was about four, Ma Sadie and Pa painted their house white. I looked at the house and thought it would look prettier with a green stripe around it. Green was my favorite color, and the house already had green shutters. I went and got the green paint out of the garage and started painting a green stripe around the house. Eventually Ma Sadie saw what I was doing. She said, "Your father's going to beat you when he comes home."

Fred Block, age fifteen months, in front of the Nathan Shain house, 1403 Chestnut Street

When Pa came home, he parked in the back yard, in the garage. When I saw him coming around the house, I started running up Chestnut Street. I got about halfway up the next block, towards downtown. He was faster than me, of course, and spanked me right there on the sidewalk. He spanked me good. Chestnut Street was a much-trav-

There were at least three "blackbirds baked in a pie" in this 1932 production by St. James Church kindergarten. Left to right (bottom row): Nell Trask, Fred Block, William Ross, Joe Morrison, and Laurence Sprunt; (top row) Fred Poisson, Francis Van Landingham, Blanche Bolles, Rockwell Poisson, and Shirley Finkelstein. (Courtesy Cape Fear Museum)

eled street in those days because the streetcar tracks went up Princess, the next street over—and Ma Sadie said a lot of people must have seen me get a spanking.

It had seemed like such a good design.

My uncle Moses Stadiem gave me a pet goose when I was five years old. That goose followed me like a dog. It never pecked me or did anything to hurt me. He wasn't a white goose, he was multi-colored. I remember I would catch him, which was easy to do. And I would turn him over on this back and pet him on his stomach—and he would let me, even though geese usually hate that.

The goose would follow me all over the yard at Chestnut Street. He had a little cage he stayed in when I wasn't there. When I was home, he was right behind me. When we moved to the beach that summer, we had a pen for him there. I'd let him out and most of the time he'd stay right around the house.

If I went to the ocean the goose would follow me out there. And he never would go out in the water. If I went in, he'd stand there and wait for me. But he followed me everywhere I went. That was the amazing thing. And if I came out the front door and he was under the house, he would come running and flying, half running and half flying, to where I was. *Honk, honk.* He would come up and nuzzle me a little bit with his bill.

Then one night my mother cooked him for dinner. The way I remember it, when I sat down at the table she told me it was my goose. I started crying. My father just said, "Oh, we can buy you another goose."

I can't remember the goose's name now. I think I buried it deep inside me. It was horrible for me to have my goose cooked—literally. It still hurts to think about him.

Aunt Miriam Stadiem, my favorite aunt, used to visit a lot when we lived on Chestnut Street. If I ever acted up, my mother would chase me up the stairs with a switch. But if Aunt Miriam was there, I'd yell for her to get behind me—and she would do her best to come between me and the switch.

But for the most part, I had a very happy childhood. The overlapping neighborhoods of Winoca Terrace and Carolina Heights were my world back then. One interesting thing is that my best friend in my early years was a girl, and her name was Elkie Burgwin. She lived next door to us at 1402 Chestnut. Her mother was very active in taking us places and doing things with us. She used to take us to the white sand pile next to Oakdale Cemetery, which was located at the southern end of our neighborhood. Just after you entered the cemetery, you could walk towards the south end of 15th Street, and there was a half a block of white sand, there on the left. We thought it was wonderful. Now they have graves in that part of the cemetery. But back then it was just an open place.

Elkie and I rode bikes together. I remember that she got an

odometer on her bike before I did—and had put many miles on it. I spent the next five years trying to catch up to her, and I don't remember if I ever did or not. But I really tried. When we would ride together, I knew we were both accumulating the same amount of miles, so I used to zigzag down the road to get more mileage. That seems like yesterday. It's very vivid in my mind.

Other than Elkie, my best friend was L. W. Fonvielle, who lived at 1510 Chestnut Street, one block away. We went a lot of places together. We studied that neighborhood and we knew every bump in the sidewalk. One day we formed a band. My father had a saxophone. I guess at one time he could play it. But I never knew how to play a saxophone.

I never took lessons. And L. W. had a trumpet, which I think he knew how to play a little bit. And Weddell Harriss had a bugle. So we all used to march around the neighborhood playing whatever

L. W. Fonvielle (left) and Fred Block, about 1936. The house in the background, 1406 Chestnut Street, belonged to Mr. and Mrs. Benjamin May.

we could think of, but none of us really knew how to play. It was just noise, but we thought we were doing something so wonderful. I'm sure it killed the people who heard us.

L. W. and I used to play dodge car. We made the game up. We would see a car coming down the street and stand on the curb, and when it got real near us we would run out and it would almost hit us. This was back in the days when you saw Model A and Model T Fords on the streets. They didn't go that fast, and they made a lot of noise.

We just did that for the sport of it. That game ended when I told Ma Sadie about it.

Across the street was a guy named Bunky White, who was younger than me. Gordon Allen, Clayton Holmes, and the Longleys were out there, too. The Longley yard on North 15th Street was sort of the mecca of the neighborhood. I was a little older than Fannie and Delean Longley. Henry Longley was still a baby. But it seemed like age didn't matter as much then. The Longleys had a swing in the yard, and all the kids used to gravitate there. Three children could sit on each side, facing each other, and swing together. We would sing—except that I can't sing. But we had fun. It was a great neighborhood.

Jocelyn Peck (Strange) and Gretter Duffy (Talbert) lived out there. I didn't know them well, but the neighborhood gave you a lot of acquaintances. Wade Harris and his brother Jim lived on 15th Street too. Wade was a little older than me, and Jim was too old for me to play with. Then there were the Romeos down the street, and the Hickses, a little further down the street. The Noes lived diagonally across the street. Thomas Darst Noe later became an Episcopal priest; so did L. W. Fonvielle. It was funny with L. W., because back when we were kids he never mentioned becoming a priest. Once we started school, he was always coming up with schemes to make money. He was always asking me, "What do you want to be, Freddie?"

And of course it was pretty well cut out what I wanted to be. And L. W. would say, "You don't have any ambition, Freddie. All you want to do is follow in your father's footsteps." And I said, "Well, it seems like a pretty good profession to me."

We would talk about it and argue about it a little bit. But we had fun.

Then L. W. and I started school together. We both were in the first grade together. Isaac Bear School was a great school. And I'll never forget. My mother took me there the first day, and the front steps were very high. Mrs. Nixon, my first-grade teacher, seemed a thousand years old. She was a small lady with glasses and was just as sweet and nice as she could be. And that first day of school, she gave me a hug and welcomed me with open arms. My mother never took me to school again. We lived about four and a half blocks from school. From that day on, I walked to school, whether it was rain, shine, whatever. It was not like it is today, where mothers have to take the children and coddle them and baby them. I got to school somehow and I got home somehow—on my own.

When it rained, sometimes the mothers would come pick up the children, but in those days there weren't many cars. The mothers would park in front of the school. There were only about ten parking places out there on Market Street, and no one ever had to double-park or anything. There was always plenty of room to park. It just shows you how few cars there were in the late 1930s.

While I was in the first grade, the teachers staged a play, and my mother coerced me into taking a part. She was very active in the things going on at school, and she came to the rehearsals for the play. I had a speaking part and I wasn't happy about it.

So finally the day came for the play. And there was my mother sitting in the audience, front and center. I started at the edge

The steps of the Isaac Bear School, located at 13th and Market Streets, could look very daunting to a first grader. The school, built in 1911–12 (shown here about 1933), existed as a grade school until 1947, when it served as the first campus for Wilmington College—now the University of North Carolina at Wilmington. Today only a back portion of the building remains. (Star-News photo, courtesy Lower Cape Fear Historical Society)

of the stage and I was supposed to hop across to the middle—and then say my lines. So I started hopping over there from the side—and I hop, hop, hopped all the way to the middle of the stage. But then I took an unrehearsed right-hand turn and I got right in front of my mother and I said, "Mama, I'm not going to do it." And then I hopped off the stage. That was the end of my theatrical career.

Years later, in 1947, I remember when Wilmington College began.

They held the first college classes at Isaac Bear School—and some of the students were sitting there in the same desks we sat in during grade school.

Above: The Longley lawn at 111 North 15th Street, with its many swings and a merry-go-round, was a favorite spot for children in Carolina Heights and Winoca Terrace. Clockwise from top right: Mrs. H. E. Longley, Delean (Gardner), Henry, Fannie (Thomason), and Betty (Turner), in the middle of the double-sided swing, about 1938. Left: H. E. Longley and son Henry (in his new cowboy outfit), about 1938. (Courtesy of Delean Longley Gardner)

UNION STATION
TO GRAND CENTRAL

My father traveled to New York City many times on business trips. He usually took the train out of Wilmington on Sunday and would come back on Friday. It was exciting taking him to Union Station. The porter came to the car at Front and Red Cross Streets and, being as we were regulars, he knew my father's name. All the porters knew my father by name.

The porter on duty would always say something like, "You going to New York again? I'll take your bags. Just let me know what compartment you got." Then he would put his luggage on a big green metal cart.

By the time we got there, the bags would be in the compartment and my father would give him a nice tip. He'd thank Pa for the tip and say, "I'll see you when you get back Friday."

Pa would return at eight o'clock Friday morning and we'd always go down and meet him. The first thing I'd ask him was, "What did you bring me?"

And he'd say, "It's in the bag. I'll give it to you when we get home." And he always brought me a present. Pa had good taste in presents because he would go to Macy's, where they devoted a whole floor to toys, things I had never seen in Wilmington. The other thing he brought back every time were foods from the delicatessen, because you couldn't buy good corned beef or good pastrami or good hot dogs here. Not like New York. They were good fat hot dogs, but full of garlic. And Pa always brought bread back because he loved good Jewish bread and you certainly couldn't buy that in Wilmington. He always said white bread was no good—"they take all the vitamins out," he believed.

The homebound train didn't leave New York until about two in the afternoon, so Pa always had a half day for shopping. He did all his business Monday through Thursday. He saved Friday morning to shop for us. Sometimes he would bring my mother a little piece of jewelry or a pocketbook. He took my mother with him to New York about once or twice a year, too. She would shop. She had a place in the Village where she bought jewelry. She would press a button and they would speak to her through a little opening in the door. The name of the jeweler was Rosenberg.

During World War II, trains were so packed Pa used to have to call Harry Stein at the Atlantic Coast Line Railroad offices to get him a ticket. The station there was so crowded, it looked like New York City. Wilmington was really a different city during the war.

Before the war, everybody knew everybody on the trains and at the depot. We always went out on the tracks to wait for my father. The place to sit was where you bought tickets, and there would be only twenty people or so in there. But during the war, you had to wait behind the gate.

KINSTON AND THE STADIEMS

As I remember, we went to Kinston a lot in those years to see my mother's family, the Stadiems. They came from Konigsburg in East Prussia. My grandmother came by way of Manchester, England, where some of the family settled and ran a clothing store. Their name was really something different. It started with an "S" and was very long, but I guess the officials at Ellis Island or wherever just gave them a new name and misspelled it.

When I was a boy, I was the only grandchild on both sides of the family. I really had it made then. Everybody would fight to play with me and buy me anything I wanted, within reason.

One of my earliest Kinston memories is the day that I was walking down the street with my grandfather Stadiem. We ran into a friend of his and he said to me in that questioning way that is really a statement, "Freddie, you know Mr. Smith?"

I answered, "No, I don't know Mr. Smith—and I don't *want* to know Mr. Smith!" I must have gotten a good scold-

Siblings Moses and Sadie Stadiem, about 1908

ing, because I remember that day so well. And I never did that again. The Stadiems kept good relations with the residents of Kinston. They knew them by name and they got a lot of return business.

My grandfather Stadiem and his siblings learned the retail business and the art of getting along from their father, David Stadiem, who was a Greensboro merchant. They became so well known that in 1926, when my parents married in Kinston, all the churches in town brought their altar flowers to my grandparents' house Sunday afternoon for them to use as wedding flowers.

When I was seven or eight years old, at Christmastime, my grandparents were so busy in the Kinston store that they would let me be cashier for small items like neckties and handkerchiefs. As I got older, I progressed to bigger items, but I started small. Christmas was always a working situation in my mother's family. They did not make any nods towards keeping the Christian holiday. Both my parents were strict about that, too with one exception. I wanted a Christmas tree so badly. All my gentile friends had them and they were so pretty. One year before I started school, my parents bought a medium-sized Christmas tree and decorated it with lights and a few ornaments. They placed it near a back wall of the living room. I guess my mother engineered it, but after that she was outvoted. My parents never had another Christmas tree.

On Sundays in Kinston, my Uncle Jake would take me out to the golf course and let me hit golf balls. My grandparents were charter members of the country club there. Jake was a pretty good golfer. He would come close to par sometimes. He could beat my father at golf. And when I went with them, I'd get about one good hit in three balls.

At other times, I would go out with Uncle Abe and Uncle Isaac and they'd show me how to play tennis. I was a better tennis player than golfer. But I was certainly not in a league with them. Abe was by far the best player, as tennis players go, but Isaac would unnerve him with a string of chatter and sort of cutesy shots with the tennis racket, almost always beating Abe. Isaac looked sort of like Jerry Springer, but he was a lot more jovial. He was the charmer.

After tennis or golf, we'd go back to the house and have a fried chicken dinner. Emma, the maid, would fry lots of chickens—about eight or ten chickens—and we had fun eating them. Each one of the Stadiems had a part of the chicken that they ate. David Stadiem was the baby and he got first choice—and he ate the breast. Isaac was sort of the next favorite, and he ate the other breast. Ma Sadie always got the wings. And the rest of them fended for themselves. When I was there, I liked the legs.

But it was always fun eating

Isaac Stadiem, Fred's uncle, ran a clothing store in Kinston and a satellite store in Wilmington.

there because there were at least twelve people around the table. My grandmother always made delicious desserts. My grandmother kept a kosher kitchen, but she ate oysters. There were always those exceptions.

During the mid-1940s, my grandmother became very sick, and we went to Kinston if not every weekend at least twice a month. The speed limits were lower because of wartime shortages. But my mother was a lead foot and really put down the gas—and we made it there in an hour and half. Ninety miles—I don't know how we didn't get caught—but I never saw a policeman. But she was a good driver. I always felt safe with her.

Sometimes my mother and I would go on Friday, and my father would come on Saturday. The trip to Kinston was something I looked forward to. I was the right age for it then. My grandparents had an old-fashioned frame house with a big wraparound porch. I was young enough to stay there and be content with the company of the Stadiems.

It was fun playing around the store. Uncle Isaac Stadiem had ladies' stores in Wilson and Wilmington. The one in Wilmington, in fact, was called "The Ladies' Store." Isaac had a wild streak to go with his charm—and his own private door into his house. He had known how to flatter since childhood, and he got by with a lot. He'd go right into the ladies' dressing rooms and ask if they needed anything. The customers would be half-clothed but he would be complimenting them so hard that most of them didn't object.

Uncle Abraham had his own men's store in Kinston. Uncle Jake and Uncle David were always at H. Stadiem in Kinston. Two of the other boys, Moses and Isaac, went to college, but my grandfather said that their education was hazardous to his business. They worked elsewhere.

One morning my father woke me up and said to me, "Get dressed, we are going to Kinston." He woke my mother up, and that was unusual because she was always up first. And she said, "What are we going over for? They didn't tell me we were going over this morning."

And he said, "Your father got sick last night. He had a heart attack and he is not expected to live. So they want us to come over." Naturally Ma Sadie cried a lot and we all got dressed. I was ten years old at the time and my younger brother, David, was only about two. When we got to Kinston, we found out that my grandfather Stadiem had died of the heart attack that night. And I always thought after that that my father knew before we got there and was trying to brace my mother for the news.

The funeral was the next day. And everybody was there. It was a huge funeral. People from all over the state came. Kinston is different from Wilmington. It's sort of in the middle of the state. It's easy to get there. People came to the store from Greensboro, Raleigh, Durham, just everywhere. There were many Stadiem relatives, descended from my great-grandfather, David Stadiem. At that time they all kept in touch.

Even after the funeral, my mother continued to go to Kinston a lot, and I was still the perfect age to go with her. My grandmother miraculously recovered. And things went along pretty well. Aunt Miriam stayed there with her and took care of her. Miriam worked in the store with David and Jake. Aunt Frances married Joe Barshay.

Uncle Isaac finally lost the Wilmington store because he didn't pay attention to his business. He wasn't like the other brothers. But no matter what, he was my favorite

Siblings David Stadiem and Sadie Stadiem Block, 1998 (photo by Susan Block)

uncle. He had such spirit. His son, William (Billy) Stadiem, is an accomplished writer who recently co-authored *Dear Senator,* the memoirs of Essie Mae Washington Williams, among other biographies.

In going to Kinston, I had lots of time to explore everything about the stores and the town. What I did mostly on weekends was go to movies. In fact, I watched one whole serial—*The Lone Ranger* or maybe *Zorro*—because we went there so often.

There was a locked door in the Stadiem house and I always wondered what was behind it. After much exploring, I finally found a key that would fit the door. It led to an attic room with lots of books, most-

Fred (left) and Nathan Block on the Stadiems' front porch, Kinston, 1942

ly schoolbooks. But it was very interesting. And there were children's clothes and toys. It was just like a little children's museum.

My Stadiem relatives never introduced me to children to play with in Kinston. What I think is that they wanted me to be their companion and be their little play toy. Once I got older, I quit going to Kinston because I had my own thing to do.

I remember that a sad event happened when I was traveling on the road. I was in Charlottesville, Virginia, and I got a telephone call that night from my mother that my grandmother had died. I was to come to Kinston as soon as I could. My mother was there when she died. She was in control of herself that time. She was prepared for the event because my grandmother had been sick so much. I got there the next day. I went to the funeral and saw all my relatives, and then I went back to Charlottesville and picked up where I left off.

I have always been proud of the Stadiems. They had great discipline. My mother and all her siblings won awards for never being tardy to school. I think all eight of them went through school without ever being tardy. And my grandfather and Uncle David and Hyman always ran the Kinston store as a model of small-town retail business.

Fred, Sadie, and David Block on the side porch on Chestnut Street, Wilmington, 1936

FLOWN FROM THE COOP

The first grade and second grade are not complete blurs to me, but I was sort of a baby. Before my brother David was born my mother kept me under her wing. Wherever she went, I went. Most places I went, she went. When I got home from school, she would say, "You're home, darling! Let's go here. Let's go there. Did you have your milk?"

She kept me sort of "babyfied" those two years. Then David was born when I was in the third grade. I'll never forget that. I was sitting in school and my teacher, Mrs. Young, came over to me and sort of whispered in my ear, "You've got a little brother. Your father's waiting outside and he's going to take you and let you see him."

I grew up that day. I really grew up that day. From then on, I was, I guess, a man. My mother transferred all the babyness to David. She stayed with him and did everything with him and for him, and sort of let me be on my own. My mother never lacked loving me, but she put all the stuff on David that she used to put on me. That was wonderful, because I would have grown up to be a big baby if she hadn't—and as it was, she let me sort of fend for myself. And David had to work out things for himself.

The day after David was born, my father put me on a train to Wilson to spend some time with relatives there. He put a tag on me that said, "Let him off at Wilson."

Miriam Stadiem, my mother's sister, was running the store in Wilson at the time. So she met me at the train. I survived. It was fun because I could tell everybody that I rode the train all by myself. Someone else from Kinston came and got me later that week. It was about Christmastime, and I spent at least a week at Wilson and Kinston.

In the third grade, it seemed like my athletic ability got better and that everything I did, I did better. I didn't know how to roller skate until then. But after David was born, somehow or another, I just let go and started skating. I remember also about that time that Elkie Burgwin moved away. Her family moved to Fifth Street. They had a house down there and they rented their house on Chestnut Street out. I really missed her when she moved, but they were only gone for a year or two. One day I saw her walking down Chestnut Street towards our house. I was on skates and I was so happy to see her. I started skating towards her and she said, "Oh, you know how to skate! You know how to skate!"

And I said, "Yes, I do." I felt so pleased that I had learned how to skate while she was away. It was wonderful having her back. She was a good friend all the way through grammar school. She was always there, and we would walk to school and back together a lot. They had programs then that I don't know if they have now—like a play at school or maybe a singalong, or just different little things. Sometimes they cost a nickel, sometimes a dime; sometimes they were free. So once a week, or twice a month, we went to those events and it was wonderful. Elkie and I could walk at night to Isaac Bear School. Nobody even thought about being afraid. We would just pick up and take off. A lot of times we met other children there, like a girl named Betty Shuman we used to visit.

There are a lot of little things I remember from grammar school days. When I was in the first grade I was maybe a little larger than most of the boys in my class. And I sort of took it upon myself to be the protector of some of the girls who were put upon by some of the older boys. I remember one morning before school, a boy named Claude Jordan—I haven't thought about that name in years—was doing something that annoyed the girls. I said to him, "You can't do that."

And he said, "I can't do that? What do you mean? I'll show you." And he started punching me, and I just beat him to a pulp. Finally the teacher, Mrs. Nixon, pulled us apart and I went into the school.

The teacher asked me, "Why did you do that?" I explained it and she said she understood.

"But look," I said. "Claude Jordan tore my shirt. Look-a there, it's all ruined."

Mrs. Nixon said to me, "Well, a shirt is the best thing he could ruin." And I guess she was right.

TRAFFIC BOY BLOCK

From the fifth to the eighth grades I was a traffic boy at 13th and Market Streets, a busy intersection right in front of the school buildings. I remember seeing a sea of people walking to New Hanover High School every day from the downtown area. A lot of families still lived down there at the time.

I walked to school every time after the first day of first grade. I walked come rain or come shine. And there were always traffic boys on the major corners going to school, to guard at crossings. You had to be in the sixth grade to be a traffic boy. So it was all I could do to wait until the sixth grade to be a traffic boy, because I thought that was the best job in the world.

I also joined so I could go to the picnic at the end of the year. The picnic was at Carolina Beach and we got out of school for the day. Policemen took us in buses and supervised. You could go into the bathhouse to change clothes into your bathing suit. They really didn't supervise us too much; they just let us out of the bus and fed us. At lunchtime, the policemen cooked hamburgers and hot dogs out on the beach. We had soft drinks. If we had our own money, we could go on the rides on the boardwalk and go inside all the little shops. It was fun. Then I'd walk home to our beach cottage, since we would usually move to the beach for the summer just before school got out.

The best intersection to be a traffic boy was 13th and Market Streets. It was very busy, and there was a policeman who stood in the middle of the street directing traffic. The southeast and the northwest corners were the best traffic boy spots. I wanted the northwest corner because it was the busiest and needed a traffic boy the most. The policeman gave it to me during the last month when I was in the fifth grade, but I couldn't keep the assignment when I was in the sixth grade because someone older than me got it.

Since I couldn't get that busy corner, I made a new corner for anyone who might want to cross on 13th Street. You really didn't need anybody there, but I wanted to be there and the policeman let me. The high school students would walk down Market Street and cross there and they didn't like to pay an attention to a little sixth-grader from Isaac Bear. I tried to get them to stop and they would ignore me, but the policeman, Mr. Wilson, told them they had to do what I said. He would blow his whistle for me when he had the time, and then the students started stopping for me. I was so proud—I would hold my little arms up there for them to stop.

Of course I knew all the grammar school students and some of the high school students, and after a while they all got to know me. I did that job in the sixth and seventh grades.

When I was in the eighth grade, my family moved to Forest Hills. I rode my bicycle to school from there and I couldn't get there by eight a.m. If you weren't a traffic boy for at least six weeks, you couldn't go on the picnic. So the last six weeks of the school year I figured out that I would take the crossing at the fire station at 17th and Dock, nearer to Forest Hills. The Pure Oil filling station, which was sort of out in the middle of the street, had a triangular plaza decorated with flowers and a statue of a little boy with a fishing rod. I could get to that crossing before the head traffic boy arrived. He started at 13th and Market, checking on all the guards, and it took him fifteen minutes to get there. I got to go on the picnic that last year.

LIFE IN A STREETCAR CITY

When I was young, Wilmington had a trolley system with streetcars and beach cars. They were all loud: *clackety-clack, clackety-clack.* The beach car came down Princess Street and made a right turn where my grandfather's house was, one lot from the corner of 17th and Princess. Then it went straight down 17th Street to about Castle Street, and on through Bellamy Park to Park Avenue. From there the beach car went all the way down Park Avenue to Wrightsville Beach.

The regular streetcar also went down Princess and turned onto 17th, where it went south past Market and turned left on Perry Avenue. Then it went down about four blocks on Perry to 20th Street, where it turned right and stopped at the end of Metts Avenue. Then it simply changed direction and came back.

When a streetcar turned around, the conductor just took the controls from one end to the other. Each end was the same, but the motorman would take the wand from the first car to the last car and rehook it to the power line above the cars.

We took our milk from Swart's Dairy because they had the freshest milk in town. The dairy was out in Castle Hayne, north of town. They had Guernsey and Jersey cows and they gave the richest milk, with lots of cream. Echo Farms, south of town, had Holstein cows that gave lighter milk, so today they would be the most popular.

On Saturday mornings, when I was eight or nine or so, the milkman would come around with an old-fashioned horse and wagon. I would ride a block or two with the milkman, and he would cover one side of the street and I would cover the other. I'd take a fresh bottle of milk to the porch and pick up the empty bottle. When we walked away from the truck to take the glass bottles, the horse was trained to walk up a house or two and wait for us. I thought delivering milk was the greatest thing.

Within three blocks of my house there were three grocery stores and two drugstores. The grocery stores were all along 12th Street: one at Chestnut, one at Princess, and one at Market. All the grocery stores sold penny candies, and about three times a week my friends and I would walk up to the store and buy candies. Sometimes we would have two or three pennies in our pocket. But when we didn't we would scour the neighborhood and look for drink bottles and milk bottles. Milk bottles we got a nickel for, and drink bottles brought two cents. We thought we were rich when we found a milk bottle, but the only ones we got a nickel for were ones that said "5 cents" on the bottle. Home delivery milk bottles brought no money, just those sold in the stores.

The only "fast food" near my house was Pete's Hotdogs and Hamburgers at 13th and Princess Streets. The Barkas family owned Pete's. The hot dogs were really good. They had chili and onions. Hamburgers were ten cents, or two for fifteen. Hot dogs were a nickel. They were the best.

We had friends close by. Bobby Bellamy lived on Market Street next to Trinity Methodist Church; we used to play football in his back yard, which went all the way to Princess Street. Bert Miars, L. W. Fonvielle, Harold Jeter, Gleason Allen, Davis Howes, George Johnson—all of us lived close and played football together. We played on Saturday mornings and sometimes during the week, in the afternoons. I was just a little thing and I'd get out there and I'd get hit, but it didn't make any difference. It was just fun playing.

Sometimes we played hockey in the street, between Princess and Chestnut, on 15th Street. Traffic was light and when a car came, we'd make them wait until we were finished with the play. We used a flattened can as the puck. Then each of us would find a long stick. We'd go up in the woods near Oakdale Cemetery and hunt for sticks. Then my father got me a better stick. He got someone at the factory to get me a special one that looked like a hockey stick. Archie McGirt, Frankie Gainey, Dolan Norris, or one of the other mechanics at the factory probably made it.

Everybody got along in our neighborhood. John Codington was part of the neighborhood. Toppy (John) Evans lived on the corner. Everybody sort of meshed together. Everybody walked. It wasn't a matter of getting your mother to take you somewhere in a car. If you couldn't walk, you just didn't go. Neighborhoods today are not that way.

In the summer, people had their windows and doors open for "air conditioning." When Mrs. Burgwin played the piano next door, we had music in our house too. Screen doors and screen windows kept out the bugs—some of the bugs, anyway.

Our neighborhood was our social club. Every Friday night, we'd get together at somebody's house. Sometimes it would be all girls in one house and all boys in another. Sometimes it would be mixed. We'd just sit there and have a good time, even if we weren't doing anything in particular.

Our gang crossed into a lot of different areas. Helen Romeo lived down the street, and so did Barbara deCover. They weren't particularly close friends, but we visited in each others' houses. Gordon Allen, who was a little younger than I was, and his brother who was a little older, lived right across the street. And sometimes Lemuel Allen would go off with his old friends, and sometimes he would stay with us and do whatever we did—which was really nothing. We would just talk and hang out together.

Sometimes we would walk up to the drugstore, one time Hall's Drugstore then another time Lane's—and then Hall's again. Hall's was between 16th and 17th, on Market Street. Old Doc Hall was really a nice man. He never called us down, even though I'm sure we annoyed him a lot.

And of course Jarman's Drug Store was there, but we didn't like Jarman's as much. Mr. Jarman was always there and he never would let us get away with anything. He was a nice man, but he'd say, "Oh no. You're not going to make all that noise."

We didn't have television in those days, so radio was the main source of news and entertainment at home. We had a radio in the living room, and sometimes we listened as a family. My father liked the news and he would go to the living room to listen after dinner. I would go to the breakfast room to do my studies. We only had one radio station in Wilmington, which didn't broadcast all day long. They were only on the air for certain hours. So we had to get programs from other places and there was lots of static.

The radios were big and stood on the floor. The dial was flat, in line with the straight front of the radio. Adults had to bend down to read it, but I remember being short enough so that it was just right. Eventually Philco designed a new front for the radio and the dial was turned up, at the forty-five-degree angle. They advertised it as "No stoop, no squat, no squint."

When I was eight or nine, I used to ride my bicycle downtown to the Royal Theater. Sometimes I'd go alone, or sometimes with L. W. or Weddell. The Royal marquee had lighted rabbits all around it. They blinked on and off at night to make it look like the rabbits were running around the sign. The Royal had a cowboy show on every Saturday.

I never went to the Bijou, the other downtown movie theater. By that time, it stank. I mean it really stank—I think old men would relieve themselves in there.

The third theater was the Carolina, on Market Street. I never went there by myself. I went there with my mother and father several times, but the Carolina didn't show the kind of movies I wanted to see at that time.

Sometimes we boys would walk up to Rose Ice, at 12th and Market Streets. They had instruments that would score the two-hundred-pound block into twenty-five- and fifty-pound blocks. The scoring blade would descend onto the big block and when it lifted, or was lifted, little pieces of ice would fall off. The boys in the neighborhood ate the little pieces.

I used to play tennis at Pembroke Jones Playground and Robert Strange Park. I was playing a lot at Robert Strange Park when I was about nine or ten years old and I got to be the seventh-ranked player. Charlie Boney was first back then; Tommy Snell was number two.

I think I would have been ranked higher, but I played with a book under my shirt. It was my Hebrew School book. I had to go to Hebrew School at the Temple of Israel every day after regular school, and I didn't want anyone to see the book. I carried the rest of my books in the basket of my bicycle. The Hebrew book had a green cover and when I sweated playing tennis, the green would rub off on my shirt. I don't think Ma Sadie ever noticed.

SET APART

I don't remember what year it started, but when I was a young boy, I attended the old synagogue on Walnut Street, between Third and Fourth streets. I went with my grandfather, William Block, who lived on Princess Street between 16th and 17th. His house was right where the streetcar came through, making a curve.

My grandfather loved me. I was the first grandchild. I was named for my grandmother, who had died not long before I was born. In the Jewish faith, children are not named for living family members. It's better that way; everyone living has a clearer identity. And there was an old saying that the angel of death might get confused about who to take back with him if there were too many people with the same name.

When children are named for those who have died, they can just use the first letter of the name. My grandmother's name was Fannie, so they named me Frederick. It wouldn't be good to name a boy Fannie. Her middle name was Leah, so mine is Lee. My cousins Franklin Block and Felice Guld were also named for her. My grandfather thought it was wonderful that I was named for her. And everything I did was just wonderful to him. I called him Mappa, and later Grandpa. He would walk to my house on Chestnut, and from there we walked together to the synagogue. That was a pretty good walk for a little kid.

The first time he just showed up and said, "Come on and walk with me?" My mother put my pretty little clothes on me, and we

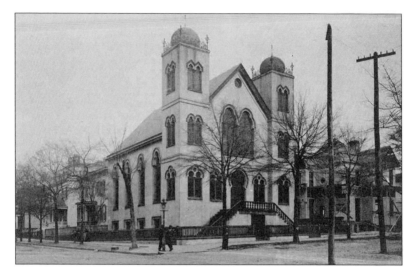

The Temple of Israel at 1 South Fourth Street, Wilmington. According to Wilmington historian Beverly Tetterton, the Temple may have been designed by architect Samuel Sloan. The William Block family lived in the house pictured at right in the early 1920s. (Courtesy Lower Cape Fear Historical Society)

walked down the street just as big as you please. Of course I was tired when we got there. I sat through the service and I didn't know what was going on. It was all in Hebrew. Mappa said, "Just sit there and be quiet." He would come sit with me sometimes, but about half the time at least he was up on the bema. He was taking part in the service.

We usually walked down Princess Street, because the sidewalks on Chestnut were not paved all the way downtown. We walked all the way there because my grandfather was an Orthodox Jew and didn't believe in riding anywhere on Shabbat. I did that from the time I was a little boy until I was at least eleven. When we got there, often the congregation would have trouble forming a minyan because there were barely enough men there. A minyan is ten men, thirteen years or older. There were eight hard-core regulars who almost never missed the service. Usually they would have to go out and find two other men.

The telephone at the synagogue was downstairs. The windows of that floor were about half above ground and half under ground. They weren't supposed to use the phone on the Sabbath, but they rationalized it was all right. And whoever was in charge that day would say, "Go downstairs and call so and so." The caller would come back upstairs and report, "Can't come today."

Most of the time they would get ten, but sometimes they would just have nine. Then they would look at me and say, "Okay, we'll count you as one." So when I was only ten or eleven, I was part of a minyan a lot of times. A little later, when I was about ten to twelve, I used to hold the weight of the Torah at the synagogue. Before that, I used to tie the string around it.

Sometimes, when they couldn't get nine adults, the congregation had a shortened service that they did without a minyan—and I used to pray for that shorter service. Instead of reading the service out loud, they would read it to themselves and they could read it faster that way. So instead of an hour service, it was about twenty minutes.

The B'nai Israel Synagogue building at 313 Walnut Street, Wilmington, served the congregation from 1913 until 1954, when members built a new structure at 2601 Chestnut Street (see page 42). (Courtesy Cape Fear Museum)

I liked that so I could get home sooner and I could go out and play. Usually, we left my house about 8:15 for the 9:00 a.m. service. Then at ten, we would go downtown for a while and I'd be back home about 11:30. When they didn't have a minyan, I got home before eleven, and it didn't take me long to find my friends because I knew where everybody was playing. It wasn't that I didn't like being with my grandfather. I loved being with him. But I wanted to get home as soon as I could.

Mr. Louis Schwartz, Mr. Abe D'Lugin, Mr. Benjamin Kingoff, Mr. Benjamin May, Mr. Abel, Mr. Cohen, Mr. Raymond Retchin, Mr. Horowitz, Mr. Jaffe, Mr. Simon, Mr. Joseph Freedland, and Mr. Neuwirth were there often. I got to be a regular, even though I didn't actually participate. My grandfather just liked to have me there with him.

Mr. Schwartz was a very devout and genuine man. He was president of the synagogue about every other year. In the alternating years, my grandfather was president.

My grandfather Block was faithful in attendance and often was the one who went seeking an extra member or two to form a minyan on Saturday mornings. He spent a lot of time every night reading his Bible. He even built a booth in his back yard every year for Sukkoth. Sometimes on Shabbat or the holiday, he'd come over to me and ask me for a light for his cigarette—because you're not supposed to light a match on a holy day.

Since the entire service was in Hebrew, I barely knew one word of what was going on at the synagogue. The pews were wooden and hard. On holy days, I would often go downstairs with friends my age. I remember Albert Levine, who later was at the Citadel with me, being there.

Sometimes at the synagogue I'd stay out as much as I stayed in. On holidays, we would walk to Saffo's store at the corner of 4th and Red Cross Streets. It would be one happy family there. You'd see young and old, and some people were eating breakfast and some lunch. I enjoyed the penny candy. You could get one piece of round chewing gum or one of the hard candies, single chocolates, or jawbreakers. It was just fun. Sometimes we'd stay out more than we stayed in.

On Saturdays at the synagogue, the men would listen to the Torah and chant, "Shema Israel!" They sang. The men really enjoyed the service. They were so happy. It made me see religion in a special way. It wasn't something you had to do; it was something that made you happy. They were so pleased doing all these things that their faces shone. They would get up on the bema and they would pray and do whatever they had to do. But when they finished, they enjoyed every little minute that they took.

When the service was over, the men would pull out some bourbon and shot glasses. They called it "schnapps," which is Yiddish for alcoholic spirits. Before and after they took a drink, they would shout in unison, "Halichey Yeddin!" There wasn't any chatter among them, but there was great fellowship.

Mr. Morris Cohen was sort of the old master. He had a long beard, and he was so old that every time he stood up I was afraid he would fall down. After the service he would take a little snuff and put it up his nose and sneeze. He was also sort of the keeper of the booze. He had a pint bottle of whisky stowed away in the synagogue, inside the lectern that was on the left-hand side, up front, near the bema.

Sometimes the rabbi, Isaac Minsky, would walk home with my grandfather and me from the synagogue on Walnut Street. He had a mustache and he lived on Princess between 13th and 14th, just about a block away from us.

Often when it was just my grandfather and me returning, we would first go downtown and visit with Mosias the tailor, in the 300 block of North Front Street. Mosias came from Riga, the same European town as my grandfather. His shop was right over Merrick's Barber Shop, where I went to have my hair cut from the time I was about three years old. We'd go up there with Mosias and sit there—and they would talk in English if it involved me. But when the two men talked, it was always Yiddish. My grandfather was a man of few words, and that's the only place I ever saw him really enjoy talking. They held memories together that others wouldn't understand.

It was just pleasant to be there with them. I would sit there and they would give me something to drink like a Pepsi, and sometimes I would eat some candy. Sometimes they would give me a book to look at or I would look out the second-story window onto Front Street. There was always a lot to see out there.

In Orthodox Judaism, you're not supposed to have any money on you on Shabbat, which is Saturday. And my grandfather would walk down the street with me and he'd look over at me and he'd say, "I'll buy you something. What do you want at the 5-and-10-cent store?" Kress's, down on North Front Street in the old Masonic Temple, was his favorite. We'd go in and he'd buy me a yo-yo or some little something. It wasn't much, but it was just the idea that he wasn't supposed to buy anything or spend any money on Saturday. He did everything right except what he did for me. It was an honor.

My grandfather never took the streetcar to or from synagogue because it went against the rules of Shabbat. One summer day it was very hot and he said to me, "I know this is too much for you. Come on. I'll take you on the streetcar home." That was a beautiful thought for him, really. His religion was so important to him, he would never do that for himself. But he loved me and felt sorry for me. In fact, taking the streetcar was doubly against the rules because you weren't supposed to take any money with you either. He almost always gave me a quarter, too.

My grandfather was usually so careful about the rules, but he loved me and he saw that as bigger than the rules. It made me love him even more. He never asked for anything; all he ever did was give. I stayed very close to him for all the years I could be with him.

Religion was a different thing in my house. My mother was a very good, very chaste woman. She did not have a passion for religion, but the conviction was there, though. She told me that when she was a girl in Kinston, a friend asked her to go to a big outdoor revival. My mother, who was about ten at the time, didn't see that it could do any harm and went along to be with her friend. At the end of the service the preacher sort of gave a twist to the old invitation to become a Christian. He asked anyone who didn't believe in Jesus to stand up. My mother stood up—the only one to do so.

After my parents were married, my mother moved our family from the synagogue to the temple because she didn't like hearing the service in Hebrew. It must have been a funny feeling for my father to leave it. I'm sure he could see the spirit in those men's faces. I would think he felt torn between my mother's wishes and his father's preference for the synagogue. But he never talked about it. I don't remember either of my parents teaching me anything directly about the Jewish religion.

I do know my father used to love to go over to my grandfather's house every night after dinner. It seemed strange to me, and it still does, that we would eat dinner at our house and then ride over there. When we got there, my father would sit in the living room and read magazines and my grandfather would sit in his room reading the Bible. They spoke when we came in and spoke when we left. And that's about all there was to it.

Usually we would stay about thirty to forty-five minutes. Even if my father and grandfather were sitting in the same room, they said little or nothing. They had some sort of camaraderie there that I never did understand. But I accepted it.

As a family, we went to the temple on Fourth Street, but then on High Holy Days, we'd go to the temple on the first day and the synagogue on the second. At the temple, you'd sit down for two hours and you couldn't move, couldn't breathe, couldn't talk, couldn't do anything. At the synagogue, you could talk while you're sitting there, or

B'nai Israel, Wilmington, today (Courtesy B'nai Israel Synagogue)

you could move around.

A different group went to the Temple of Israel from those who attended the synagogue. There were only a few families there then, but they were strong ones. The Bluethenthal, Jacobi, Solomon, Sternberger, and Bear families *were* the temple at that time, in the 1930s and 40s.

At the synagogue on Walnut Street, everything was done the real old-fashioned Orthodox way. They even had a mitvah in the basement. I guess it was very popular when indoor plumbing was scarce, but it was seldom used by the time I was a boy. A mitvah is a ceremonial bath women were to take every month. Just before women got married, they always went to the mitvah to be ceremonially clean. My father's favorite joke, which I remember hearing from the time I was three years old, was that he wanted to be a lifeguard at the mitvah.

There was never a woman at the synagogue on Saturday morning. The women would come on Friday nights and holidays. They sat upstairs and they dressed to the nines, and all they did was talk. I guess some of them knew how to read Hebrew, but you'd look up there and all they did was yak, yak, yak. They had a ball. It was a social thing for them. It was always full. It was never empty up there in the "rafters," as we called it. The only time they'd be quiet was when the rabbi was giving a sermon. They gave him that courtesy, but he would have to hit his hand on the book and look up there and say, "Yaah, yaah, yaah!"

But I *loved* that synagogue.

MA SADIE AND FREDDIE BOY

Before I was born, my parents were neighbors of artist Claude Howell, who lived in the Carolina Apartments at Fifth and Market when my parents still lived in the first block of South Fifth Street. Claude and my father's niece Shirley Block became great lifelong friends. One day in 1927, Ma Sadie, Claude, and Shirley were taking a walk. On the spur of the moment, Shirley and Claude decided to run around the block, something they customarily did. My mother, pregnant with me at the time, ran with them—and about halfway, she fainted. She had always been very athletic and it never occurred to her that she shouldn't run in that condition.

One night when she was nearly eight months pregnant, my mother was at the temple with my father. They heard the sirens coming from the fire station down that block, and my mother had a premonition that it was the shirt factory on fire. (That was the factory on Hanover Street, between Third and Front, that we were leasing from the Bear family. There was a Nehi bottling plant there too. My father and the manager of the Nehi place used to have schnapps together after work, much to my mother's dismay.)

Someone came rushing into the temple to get my father: the factory *was* on fire. He rode with someone, then my mother got a ride, too. Even in her condition she ran down the cobblestone street beside the old factory on North Front at Hanover. She had to get to her Nathan.

My mother may have ridden with someone to the fire that night, but she could drive. I remember her telling me how she drove her family up north when she was just fifteen years old. They had a touring car called an Apperson Jackrabbit, with translucent windows that could be removed. She and her eight siblings were getting out of the car one day and a stranger asked if it was an incubator.

After the fire in the factory, the lease had some time remaining on it and they fixed the building up so that the company could get back into it. Meanwhile, my father bought the old Wilmington Printing business that fronted on Greenfield Street between Second and Third. We moved over in the 1930s. I don't remember the old factory, but I have many memories of the one on Greenfield.

At the Hanover Street factory, they were producing about 100,000 dozen shirts a year, but they weren't making any boys' shirts at the time. The finest shirt the company made was called Sir William,

named after my grandfather.

Then I came along. My father and grandfather were so happy that they closed the factory for the day on November 17, the day I was born. "Now that we have a grandson, we're going to name a shirt 'Freddie Boy,'" they said. I wish I had one of those labels. They were the cutest little things you ever saw. The name was in script, underlined by the tail of the "F."

Some of the older people at the factory called me Freddie Boy. A lot of them called me Freddie even after I was running the place. It never seemed disrespectful. They had earned the right through seniority. I enjoyed my time in the factory when I was a boy, and it felt like home.

This aerial view of the Block Shirt factory was probably taken about 1938, when it was located in the 200 block of south Greenfield Street. The entrance was moved to 1510 South Third Street about 1948, when a new wing was added. (Courtesy Cape Fear Museum.) Below: Advertisement for Block shirts

SPORTS IN THE 1930S

In the 1930s, the major league sport of interest for us was baseball. Of course there was no television then. During the World Series, the owner of the *Morning Star* constructed a large wooden board outside the newspaper offices in the Murchison Building at the corner of Front and Chestnut Streets as a way of indicating the action as it was happening miles away and reported on radio.

That was one time my mother did go out of her way to transport me. After school, she would drive me downtown and drop me off around the post office. I would stand with hundreds of people watching and listening to the World Series. The board was constructed and wired so that when a batter hit the ball, a ball would go into the area where the real hit went. If someone got on base, the board would show a runner standing on the base. If it were an out, it would show that the person hit the ball, and then you could see that it was caught. If someone got a hit or did something really good, the crowd on the street would cheer and clap.

Then my father would pick me up on his way home from work.

I remember when Babe Ruth was hitting and Lefty Grove was pitcher for the Yankees. Bill Dickie was the catcher for the Yankees. Lou Gehrig was at first base. The famous manager at the time was Joe McCarthy of the Yankees. Bob Feller was pitcher for the Cleveland Indians.

I bought baseball cards, which came inside bubble gum wrappers. I also played sandlot baseball. In those days, you didn't specialize—you played whatever sport was in season. During baseball season, all the people in grammar school who wanted to

During the 1930s, spectators stood across the street at 200 North Front Street to watch the baseball board in front of the Murchison Building (at right). According to the Morning Star, *September 28,1927: "World Series games which start next Wed. in the city . . . will be played in Wilmington on the most approved magnetic board that science has yet evolved which will be erected in front of the Morning Star building. Work on the erection of the scaffold will start immediately. The board will be elevated above the height of the second floor of the building." If a streetcar or automobile happened along, recalls Fred Block, "you just had to wait." (Courtesy Lower Cape Fear Historical Society)*

play would meet at Pembroke Jones Playground across from New Hanover High School. The grammar-school children would pick up sides. The baseball diamond was behind the tennis courts, next door to St. Andrew's Presbyterian Church.

When I first started going over there, the park was kept very pretty. They had flowers all around and nice little paths. Black maids called "nurses" by their employers, were there with the little children they were looking after. The nurses would talk together and the children were playing all over the place. When I was about ten or eleven, they used to have a softball game between the men teachers in high school and the students—in Pembroke Jones Park. It's interesting to remember that the teachers got a free beer whenever they hit a home run.

From the time I was about ten until I was thirteen, I thought playing football would be wonderful. We got out of Isaac Bear School at 2:15 in the afternoon, but the high school football players got out earlier and would dress in their uniforms and sort of jog down Thirteenth Street. It seemed like the most romantic thing, to see the uniformed players going to practice. Some days we would ride our bikes down to the fields and sit there and watch them for a while.

I was on the eighth-grade football team at Isaac Bear, but I had to quit because my mother wanted me to go to Hebrew School. I couldn't do both. That was the year of my bar mitzvah, so I had to go to the synagogue to study. The temple didn't have a good program at that time.

After that I got on the football team at New Hanover. As a freshman, I was on the third team. But my mother made me quit that, too, because I didn't get home from practice until after dinner. Dinnertime was very important in my house. We were all sitting at the table at six o'clock sharp. My father would sit down and eat. He wasn't interested in conversation at the table. He just ate—and he ate fast. Dinnertime was regimented and mandatory when I was growing up, but food was and is a very happy part of my life.

Fred (back) and David Block, about 1938. The house in the background, 1407 Chestnut Street, belonged to William A. McGowan.

FOOD CUSTOMS IN THE BLOCK HOUSEHOLD

My mother loved to grocery shop. She was a good shopper, and she taught me how to pick out good produce and meats. I watched her cook and learned that too. Once, when I was fifteen, she went to Florida for ten days—I think she went with the Stadiems. It was my job while she was gone to plan the meals, shop, and cook for my father, David, and me. The maid was going to help me, but she got sick. It was during the war, and everybody had meat ration coupon books. I bought what I could, and I remember that we had lamb chops and steak.

My father was really raised to be religious, but not my mother— they didn't have a rabbi half the time in Kinston. Among the Stadiems, Moses was the only really religious one. He went to all the services and always had the seder.

We didn't keep exactly kosher in our household in Wilmington, but my parents tried harder when my grandfather came to live with us after he and his second wife, Lena Wolk, split up. Lena and my grandfather went to Riga after they were married, to see the family there. He enjoyed that trip, though he really wasn't much of a traveler. She loved going places. And now, looking back, I can see that there were many family pressures on her. After they separated, he didn't have anyone to keep house for him, so he and my Uncle Joe came and lived with us.

Aunt Esther and Uncle Moe Guld lived in Portsmouth, Virginia back then. Moe and his two brothers had a shoe store there, but when the Depression came along and there wasn't enough business for all three, Moe came to Wilmington to work for us as a salesman.

So Grandpa Block came to live with us, and he was a very religious man and he kept kosher. We never observed it as well as he would have liked us to. But we did keep kosher meat and observed about ninety percent of food customs. That was before they had freezers for grocers to freeze meat and send it around the country. So at the time, the only kosher meat in Wilmington was at the City Market, where they would butcher the cows weekly. A man named Holland from Brunswick County brought kosher meat to the City Market.

Kosher means "clean." But the City Market was the dirtiest thing I had ever seen in my life. It looked bad and smelled worse. There were flies and other terrible things on the meat. At the time, there were maybe ten different stalls for local butchered meat. They had one stall for kosher, and the meat there was cheaper than what the grocery stores sold because the market venders were local. I guess these were all old milk cows that were slaughtered for meat when they stopped giving milk—and they were tough. My God, that meat was tough.

Somehow or another we survived the beef. It exercised our teeth a lot. My mother could season it up and cook it all day long. Even if it was tough, it tasted pretty good by the time my father got home for the meal that night. Sometimes Ma Sadie was lucky enough to buy liver. Since there's only one liver in each animal butchered, it generally went to the first customer to get there. But now that I know what the liver does, I'm not so sure that was a good thing.

Kosher chickens were supposed to be killed by the rabbi. The rabbi had a special way he killed chickens. He had a knife, a very sharp knife. Jewish cooks pick chickens dry; they don't put any water on them. Then they salt them and you're not supposed to eat them for twenty-

Wilmington artist Claude Howell depicted the City Market vegetable vendors in oil (above) and crabmeat pickers in charcoal (below; private collection).

four hours. But Holmes, the butcher, learned to do this because there weren't any Jewish chicken killers in Wilmington. He learned to cut their throats like the rabbi did.

Holmes had hundreds of chickens in his store on Dock Street, between Front and Second. There were just two fresh chicken businesses, Holmes and Von Oesen. But Holmes was the only one Jewish people dealt with. My mother didn't like the chickens at the A&P, which she called "cold storage chickens." At Holmes, she actually picked out the chickens she wanted him to kill for her. He would pick out a hen and she'd say, "That hen's too old. Get me a young one."

We always bought eggs from somebody in the country because my mother wanted them to be fresh. Sometimes she would buy them from Holmes because he had eggs brought in from the country.

We used to keep chickens in the backyard, too. At one time we had white leggings—they were the best laying hens. And then we had Rhode Island Reds, and a Dominique that was multicolored. My mother worked it out with the rabbi to kill the chickens we raised.

We'd get a few eggs from the chickens. We'd grow the chickens and when they got big enough for fryers, we'd kill them and eat them. My mother would get Louise Green, the maid (who lived close by, at 107 South 12th Street) to take two chickens over to the rabbi's house that was behind ours. Maybe there was a hundred yards between our back doors. She'd carry the chickens in her arms. Sometimes I didn't like the way she carried them—she would hold them by the feet and they would hang their heads down. But most of the time I wouldn't let her do that because I was afraid they suffered.

We'd get over there and the rabbi would have that razor-sharp knife. After he said a prayer for the chicken, he would hold it and pluck out two or three feathers from the neck so he could see where he was cutting. And he would hold it firmly and cut—and blood would squirt at least six feet because he would hit the jugular every time. The blood came out with a sound like *sshhhh*. The rabbi would hold the chicken until it quit bleeding, and then drop it on the ground. It would jump two or three times before it was officially dead.

Eventually Louise learned to kill the chicken and drain it the same way, so my mother did not send any more of them to the rabbi. I think

Louise skipped the prayers. My mother always had the chicken killed on Friday morning, because Jews eat chicken on the weekend—on Sunday.

Rabbi Minsky killed the cows that were sold as kosher beef at the City Market. He also killed chickens once a week for everybody else at the Holmes Poultry Company, then Holmes would dress them for the Jewish community. I remember Mr. Holmes being there all the time in the midst of his chickens—waiting for someone to choose one for their next meal. What a life he had.

Kosher chicken is a treat. It really does taste better than regular chicken because of the bleeding. The rabbi would hang them up until every drop was gone. You'd never see brown- or black-looking bones. It just tastes better. In most major restaurants in New York, they use kosher chickens.

We had fish on Shabbat, every Friday night. My mother lit candles. Ma Sadie bought the fish from a woman named Mrs. McCormick at the City Market. My mother loved her. And then later, she bought fish from Zora's on Castle Street. Usually, when we shopped in town, she bought flounder. But sometimes it was trout.

We always had lots of fresh vegetables and fruits. My mother bought a lot of them at the City Market. That part of the market was relatively clean. The people who sold produce always hawked their wares as we walked through. They all knew my mother. She would examine every little piece before she bought anything. You could also buy little homemade cakes there. Some ladies made them at their homes and brought them down there every weekend. They were shaped sort of like cupcakes and were very good.

SUMMERS AT CAROLINA BEACH

My mother saved five hundred dollars out of her household budget to build a two-bedroom summer cottage at Carolina Beach, a popular summer vacation spot a few miles south of Wilmington. The house didn't sit very high, just high enough to have a garage and a maid's room underneath. It was just past the lake, at the far south end of what was Carolina Beach in those days. There were no houses between our house and Wilmington Beach. There was a log cabin about a block away, in Wilmington Beach. That was the closest house to ours on the south side.

I enjoyed watching the crew build the house. To level the lot, a man brought a mule with a scoop. He would take the scoop and fill it up with dirt or sand. Then when it was filled he would let the mule pull it to the part where he wanted to dump the sand. The scoop was approximately six feet long, three feet wide, and about a foot deep. The part that scooped was flat and he would dump it, pull it back to the place he started, and get another scoop.

I remember my mother wanted a screened porch—and she had her screened porch all the way around the front, back, and one side of the house. She wanted it wide enough for people to sit there comfortably and not have to sit sideways, so it was a good, wide porch. We ate every meal on the back porch. That was where our dining room was, and we had it wide enough so that we had plenty of room to eat out

Nathan and Sadie Block at the "Please Don't Rain House" on Carolina Beach,
about 1934

there. The prevailing wind didn't blow that way, so usually we could
even eat there in the rain.

We had a closed-in chicken coop under the house. Ma Sadie
would buy fryers and hens from Holmes Poultry and keep them there.
And whichever one she wanted, she would send Louise to kill them.

One day Louise cut the chicken's throat but didn't quite cut it deep enough, and the chicken jumped up and ran away. There was a big pile of woods right to the north, near the house, that you really couldn't get into because it was marshy. The chicken ran there and we couldn't get in to get her.

The chicken survived and kept coming over to our house to eat food. We'd always open the door and hope to get her into the coop, but we never could catch her. The next year, that chicken was still there when we came down in the summer. And every time the chicken would lay an egg, she would cackle like hens do when they are ready to set. We didn't have a rooster, though, and the eggs must have rotted away. But the chicken stayed that whole summer.

Later, my father's brother Charlie and his wife, Hannah, built a house on the ocean, and we were one house back. My father and Charlie bought the two lots because there was supposed to be a lakeside luxury hotel in the works. The developers never built the hotel. They built the help quarters—the maids' and butlers' wing. It stood there for years, one long building on the western side of the lake, until it finally burned down.

Hannah was a native of Portsmouth, Virginia, who was living in New York City when Charlie met her. I remember when I first saw Hannah, right after they were married. She was very striking. She had been a singer in New York who went by the stage name Nina Rhodes. At Carolina Beach she was a lifeguard, and she trained many young people there to be lifeguards. Hannah and Charlie's first child, my cousin Franklin, was born in 1936. Mary came a few years later. Hannah was a different kind of Block at the time. The rest of the family either worked at the factory or worked in the home, but Hannah was interested in civic affairs. She still is today, in her nineties.

My father might have found the real estate for the beach house, but my mother is still the reason we had the house. She was very good at saving money. She started a bank account and saved the five hun-

Miriam Stadiem, Sadie's sister and Fred's favorite aunt, about 1933

dred dollars in it by economizing on this and that, over a three or four year period. There was a carpenter from Kinston named Mr. Carroll Hahn, and both my parents knew him. I think in those days you had carpenters, but you had very few contractors. And he told my parents, "I can build you a house. If you've got $500, I can build you a house on that lot down there."

She gave it some thought and talked to my father about it. And Mr. Hahn built the house. It *was* a house, but you could see through the boards in it. When the wind would blow, you had to get out of the way. We spent summers down there for about eight years. And when it rained, you had to put pots under the leaks in the roof. Ma Sadie called it the "Please Don't Rain House."

After my grandfather's divorce—when he and Joe came to live with us on Chestnut Street—they also came along with us to the beach in the summer. My grandfather had one of the two bedrooms. My parents and David had the other bedroom. I slept on a daybed in the living room. And my father closed in the end of a porch and made a bedroom for Joe, which was very small. After they left, the porch became my bedroom.

Things were so different then. People didn't stay in motels or rent apartments like they do now. There was no question but that people who came to see us would stay with us. The Kinston Stadiems visited frequently, and we made room. Miriam Stadiem lived with us for a while. So did Ellis Fried, one of William Block's nephews from Baltimore.

At other times, my mother's aunt and uncle would visit from Greensboro. This was probably one of the

Fred Block at Carolina Beach, where the fishing was easy, about 1937

strangest things that ever happened at our beach house. Aunt Sadie Stadiem and Uncle Abe Stadiem were my mother's father's brother and sister. They were very small, short people. Sadie was a half a head taller than Abe, but still tiny. Neither of them ever got married, and they lived together their whole lives. They had their own ways and were sort of peculiar, but were good people.

My father and mother saw them occasionally when they went to Greensboro. So one day, we were sitting on the back porch at Carolina Beach, facing the road. We were right on the highway. And a Trailways bus pulled up. We were sitting there watching and all of a sudden these two short people, both of them with hats on, got off the bus. They had these funny looking cardboard suitcases, and they looked like they had just gotten off a boat. And the bus pulled away and we looked again: it was Aunt Sadie and Uncle Abe! They had come to visit but they hadn't told anybody. They just hopped up and came down to Carolina Beach. My mother was happier about it than my father was.

Aunt Sadie was a cleanliness freak. She and Uncle Abe came into the house, and she hadn't been there five minutes when she grabbed a broom and started sweeping out the beach cottage. And at the beach, you can always get sand off the floors. She just had the best time sweeping up that sand and throwing it out the door.

They stayed about a week and a small house suddenly felt like a *very* small house.

At Carolina Beach, there were vegetable, fish, and ice vendors that came around every morning. In those days, there were three competing ice companies: Rose Ice Company, Independent Ice Company, and Plate Ice Company. They used to come down the highway calling "Ice Man! Ice Man!"

Most days they would come along together, one after the other. And one was always trying to get ahead of the other. For some reason, I always preferred the Independent Ice Company. My mother liked Plate. When they'd come down the street, I'd try to get the Independent man to come there because I thought they gave us the biggest piece of ice. She thought the Plate man did. We bought ice from the iceman the whole time we lived there, with the possible exception of the last year when we got an electric refrigerator. The ice block went in the top of the icebox, where it gradually melted and drained out a tube through the floor to the outside. When you got a drink, you would take the ice pick and cut off a piece of ice and put it in your drink. It was pretty clever in that simple sort of way.

The ice lasted from one day to the next, and the iceman came every morning to put a new piece in the icebox. The pricing of the ice was a very inexact science, and my mother knew that. She would look at them and say, "Oh, we got some ice left over from yesterday. We'll only need a fifteen-cent piece today."

Sometimes she would say, "Oh, today we need a twenty-five-cent

The fishermen of Seabreeze, a community just north of Carolina Beach, brought their catches to a waiting clientele and an eager audience. The tanned little boy just to the left of the propeller (sitting on the dark green boat) is Fred Block. Others include Ben Willis (dark trunks, on left) and Agnes Peschau (in white, between the two fishermen). (Photo probably made by John Hemmer; courtesy New Hanover County Public Library)

piece." It would be her decision, and if they didn't bring her what she thought was the right size piece, she'd say, "Now you know that's not a twenty-five-cent piece! Now you go out and you bring me more ice in here." The prices ranged from a dime to a quarter, but she was really tough on those ice people.

And then we had the vegetable vendors who also came every morning. One man, "Watermelon Joe" Howard, would sing, "I got 'em, I got 'em. I got fresh beans, I got fresh peas, I got everything."

And some days, when he'd been gigging the night before, he'd say, "I got fresh fish." The flounder he caught and sold was some of the best fish I've ever tasted. Somehow or another he kept it very cold. Later on they had vendors that just sold fish, but it was never as good as the fish Mr. Howard sold.

One of the things that I remember most was Mr. Freeman's fishing boats that came from Seabreeze. Mr. Freeman and all the people who worked for him were black. They had lived there at Seabreeze, a beach community for African Americans, for a long time. Mr. Freeman's men were hard workers, and consistent. There were three fishing boats, all painted forest green at that time. Anywhere from one to three boats went out every day. Each was manned by two to three men. They docked behind Fergus Seafood Market, a block south of the Pavilion on Carolina Beach.

There was only one outboard motor between the three boats, and most mornings the boat with the outboard motor would pull the other two boats along with it. They would go to a special spot off Fort Fisher and fish from daybreak until early afternoon, and then they would go back to their spot behind Fergus Fish Market to sell their catch. As a young boy, I would go with my mother several days a week to buy very fresh fish. We would watch the ocean from our porch and wait to see when the boats would return. They sailed back because the prevailing wind was from the south. The billowing sails were visible for miles.

Part of the excitement of the day was watching them beach the boats. They had to come through the breaking surf, a difficult task. People from the beach would stand around and help the fishermen pull the boats up onto the shore. Two men would take an oar and put it through a rope attached to the bow of the boat and they would lift up the bow and pull, and all the other people would push the boat onto shore. It was a child's delight to help beach the boats.

Then everyone would start buying fish from the boats. The greatest majority of the fish were black bass. But there were also redmouths, pigfish, flounder, croakers, trout, and spots. But flounder was the prize. That was the favorite, and the customers tried to grab them first.

All the fish were put in bunches priced at twenty-five cents a bunch and tied together, anywhere from two to four fishes, with sea oats. People would gather around the boats and pick out the bunches they wanted and give them back to the fishermen to be cleaned and filleted and washed. The fishermen didn't even charge extra for that. I never remember them coming in without plenty of fish to sell. It's amazing but one quarter bought our family of four plenty of fish for dinner—and they were *such* good fish!

We'd go up there at least twice a week. My mother would say, "I want that one! I want that one!" She fought for the ones she wanted. She was a feisty woman. She was tough. I was with her and she would show me a good one and say, "Try to get that one over there." And I'd try to get that one.

We'd take the fish home, and we'd cook them when my father came home. We lived at Carolina Beach in the summer from the time I was in the first grade until the eighth grade. We moved there and back according to the school calendar.

At Carolina Beach we lived on a dead-end street, a gravel street that never was paved. Some young men and women would use it as a lovers' lane. They would park out there and my mother would take it on herself to go out and yell to them. "This is not the place to do that sort of thing," she would say. "I've got young children here that don't need to see that." That was the same kind of thing she did when my Aunt Miriam stayed with us on Chestnut Street and would stay out in Joe Friedman's car a minute too long.

It's funny—I don't remember any of the people who came there to park getting stuck in the sand. But in the daytime, especially on weekends, people would get their cars stuck. They were usually sightseers who would just drive out on the gravel and make a three-point turn to go back the other way and would get stuck when they got off into the soft sand. They would want to use our phone, but we didn't have one. My parents would go out there and help them get unstuck. My mother was good at that. It was an art. She would drive their car out of the sand. My father would direct the people to push and he would kind of push or make like he was pushing. He didn't want to hurt his back. It was something to do on Saturday or Sunday afternoons—to get drivers unstuck.

I used to bowl with my father at night on the boardwalk. I could beat him. In the afternoons, I would walk down to the boardwalk to buy a comic book or something and one day I made a deal with the man at the bowling alley. If I set up my own pins, I could bowl free in the day. I got lots of practice. It was an open-air alley.

Usually I went barefooted the entire time we were living at Carolina Beach. I took off my shoes when we first got to the cottage and I didn't put them back on until we left to move back home. Sometimes the sand and the boardwalk would burn the bottoms of my feet, but I didn't care. I was at the beach.

The summer of 1940, my parents sold our house on Chestnut Street while we were living at Carolina Beach. That was the next to last summer we spent down there. They got a good price for the house on Chestnut. But it was a little premature, and we didn't have anywhere to live at first when we moved back to town.

MOVING

My mother wanted to move to a farm we had at Scotts Hill—way up in the northern part of the county—and I didn't want to do that. Can you imagine being in the eighth grade and stuck out in the woods with no car—and riding into town every day?

Anyway, when we had to move, my father got together with his brother Charlie and they worked out a deal so that we lived with Aunt Hannah and Uncle Charlie in the suburb of Forest Hills the year I was in the eighth grade. It worked out. My father said no two women could ever live in the same house. My mother said, "I'll prove that you're wrong"—and she did.

We survived a year there, and it was very pleasant. Usually after dinner both couples would take a ride somewhere. Occasionally they all went together, but usually they drove separately. My parents liked to go to movies, or they visited my grandfather on Princess Street or sometimes their close friends Minnie and Harry Stein on North 15th. I was thirteen years old and the chief babysitter for my brother David and my cousin Franklin. David was six years old and Franklin was three. It was fine during the week, but I wanted to go out every weekend and just go *out on the town*. We worked out a deal where I would go out on Saturday nights, and sometimes when my parents came home from temple on Friday nights, I'd go out then too.

I had my bar mitzvah while we lived there with Hannah and Charlie, so I studied a lot while I was babysitting. I also studied with Rabbi Harry Bronstein at his house on Chestnut Street between Fourth and Fifth Streets. But the actual service was a quiet affair, and the reception was low-key. Both took place in the ground floor room of the synagogue. Ma Sadie always said she would have given a bigger party if she'd had her own kitchen to cook in.

We lived with Hannah and Charlie from the time school started in 1940 until late September 1941. I got to know Forest Hills and know the area. It was very different than living on Chestnut Street, because things were much further apart. I made friends with Graham Barefoot, Louis Hanson, Raymond Thomason, and Charlie Mitchell—and a lot of other people there.

But there was a lot of sadness, too, because I had to give up some of my other friends. You couldn't have but so many friends if you couldn't get to see them. It was geographic. When you are young, your friends are where you live.

So if you don't have a car, what are you going to do? We couldn't snap our fingers and get our mothers to take us. Mothers just didn't carry children around like they do today. You got where you were going by yourself. You rode your bicycle. I rode my bicycle from Hannah's house to Isaac Bear School virtually every day of the eighth grade. It was a pretty good trip. Come rain or come shine, I made my way. I figured out how to get there in the rain and I figured how to get there in the shine.

One friend of mine, Louis Hanson, lived on Colonial Drive. We would meet on the corner of Metts Avenue and Forest Hills Drive, where Walker Taylor lived. Louis and his father would drive up there. I don't know why his father did it and I don't know why we did it or why my mother let me do it (I don't think she knew)—but we'd hold on to Mr. Hanson's car and he would drive down Metts Avenue and we wouldn't have to pedal our bikes. And he'd take us all the way down to 17th and Dock, where he dropped us off. And then he'd go on down

*From left: Fred, Sadie, David, and Nathan Block at 711 Forest Hills Drive,
Wilmington, about 1941*

to his office, which was on the way. We'd ride the rest of the way to
school. Towing bicycles like that was so dangerous. But you have no
fear when you're in the eighth grade. We had a very nice time.

My parents were building a new house at 711 Forest Hills Drive.
Ma Sadie was very excited, but Pa was about a tenth as excited. The
thing was, we had just been through a depression and money was tight.
My father was still paying off the mortgage on the house on Chestnut
Street when he sold it. He used the proceeds towards the new house.

On a trip we took to the World's Fair in 1939, my parents first saw
a house like they wanted to build. Unfortunately, my father cut some
corners to save money. He reduced the size of the entire house and he
cut the ceiling height down by a foot. And he changed the plans for
the basement. At first he didn't even put an outside entrance to the
basement—that was done later. And the heating system was not
intended to be exposed. And then the garage was changed; it was supposed to be built under the first floor. The garage we had has now been

redone as part of the interior of the house, by the Easons, the way the original plans dictated. There have been only three owners of the house: my parents, the D. M. Lamdins, and now William and Marie Eason.

Some things changed after we moved to Forest Hills. My parents had both been raised kosher, and as long as we lived on Chestnut Street I don't remember ever having bacon. But some- how when we moved to Forest Hills Drive, bacon started making its way to our table. I don't know how they worked that out. Also, we had fish on Shab- bat when I was young, and that changed over the years, too.

One thing I enjoyed on Forest Hills Drive

Fred Block at 711 Forest Hills Drive, 1941

were the ducks and geese we raised in the back yard. The yard was big and we decided to block it off into sections, or strips, that led to the railroad tracks. The part nearest the house was reserved for shrubs and flowers. The middle part was a large greenhouse made of lath. And the section nearest the tracks was for the ducks and geese and chickens. We had a fence so that the birds wouldn't wander out onto the tracks.

Every morning we would wake up to hear *honk, honk, quack, quack*. And I kept up the ducks and geese for years. I even bought an incubator. Everything I heard said you only raise about twenty-five percent of ducks and geese. So I had room for fifty eggs in the incuba- tor, and I filled it up. My first hatching, I got forty-seven ducks and geese. So we had a whole yard of them. They are not like chickens; chickens don't take up much room. But a big old goose will take a lot

J. E. NEWTON AND SON

GENERAL CONTRACTORS AND BUILDERS
BUILDERS OF FINE RESIDENCES
AND
COMMERCIAL BUILDINGS

FLOOR FINISHING
CONCRETE WORK
ROOFING

DIAL PHONE 4906

BRICK WORK
STORE FRONTS
REMODELING

INSULATION
STAIR WORK
PAINTING

P. O. BOX 1316

WILMINGTON. N. C.

December 10, 1940.

Mr. Nathan Block,
City.

Dear Sir:

We have very carefully examined the plans and specifications for
your proposed residence to be built in New Forest Hills and we agree for the
sum of Thirteen Thousand Eight Hundred Seventeen &no/100 Dollars ($15,817.00)
according to the plans and a revised specification to be furnished. The
principle changes in the original plans and specifications are as follows:

(1)- No terrace is to be built on the rear of the house.
(2)- The basement laundry along with the outside stairway and
iron handrail to same is omitted. The laundry tray is to be
set in the garage ; a wood top is to be provided for the tub.
(3)- All curtain walls and basement walls are to be of 8" brick masonry.
(4)- All lumber is to be of #2 Com grade in all framing work. Framing
etc to be same as that of F. E. Newtons house in Sunset Park.
(5)- All Footings are to be of concrete 8"x20" with three ½" steel
reinforcing rods in same. Basement walls and floor is to have no
reinforcing steel.
(6)- Roof is to be covered with Ruberoid Eternit Dutch-Lap Asbestos
Shingles.
(7)- All gutters and downspouts are to be of 26Ga. Galv Iron. Valleys
and flashings to be of 16 oz copper where same are so placed as
to make future renewal dificult.
(8)- Front porch columns are to be square local make.
(9)- The following allowances have been made for the purchase of the
items listed below:

(a)-Iron balcony on rear—	$ 100.00
(b)-Medecine cabs————————	40.00
(c)-Hardware ———————————	125.00
(d)- Kit. Linolium————————	50.00
(e)-Electrical Work complete—	235.00
(f)- Plumbing Complete————	950.00
(g)- Heating Complete————————	900.00

We trust that this bid may be found satisfactory and that we will be
favored with this contract, we are

yours very truly,

J. E. Newton & Son,

By

(This bid is for immediate
acceptance sothat protection
can be secured on the materials
to be used on this job)

We carry workmens compensation and public liability insurance for the protection
of our customers.

A bill for construction on the Blocks' Forest Hills home, 1940 of room. The next time I got over forty ducks and geese again. We had enough of them forever. I had a funny habit of naming animals after our family and acquaintances. So we had a Sadie; a Nathan; an Oscar after Oscar Glick, a salesman; and a Bert after salesman Bert Frey. And we had a goose named after a nervous friend. We named only the geese—the ducks didn't have near the character a goose had. And a goose egg was about twice the size of a chicken egg. My mother loved to bake with goose eggs because she only had to use one egg for a recipe.

At the same time, Jere Freeman was raising bantam chickens up the street. He gave me two of them. Bantams are interesting because they can fly like regular birds. They could take off from the house and fly to the chicken coop at the bottom of the hill. During my first years of living on Forest Hills Drive, Wrightsville Beach became a big thing to us. It was the place to go. I remember the Landis Cottage at Wrightsville Beach was a good place to hang out when I was at New Hanover High School. The elder Mrs. Landis had a granddaughter named Carrie May Wade. A lot of the people who stayed there were friends of Carrie May and the Wades, wherever they were from. They would bring girls down to the beach, and they had a place the girls stayed on the first floor called the Bull Pen. It was all innocent and above board, but the charming, pretty girls drew lots of attention.

After we moved, my father worked out something with Merrick's Barber Shop to get our haircuts. It was so crowded down there during the war that we had to wait and wait. Alonzo Farnsworth was one of their barbers, and I think he was a relative of theirs. He started coming to our house on Sundays to cut hair. He cut my father's hair, and mine, and David's. He would bring long matches and burn the ends of our hair. He said all the old barbers had passed down word that it made hair thicker. We all loved Alonzo, who lived next to the corner at Eighth and Dawson Streets.

SHIRT TALES

In 1941, the year I turned fourteen, the Block company was having trouble with the amalgamated CIO union. They wanted us to sign a contract with the union, and my father didn't want to do that. So around the Fourth of July that year, they went on strike. About half the pressers, who were all black, went out and maybe a quarter of the white workers went out. They set up a picket line out in front of the building. They had people marching in the picket line with signs, and they would harass the employees as they came in to work and people who came in to deliver things. And we had plenty of people working. People were looking for jobs then, and as soon as the ones on strike quit working, the company hired new employees.

Block was the first company in Wilmington to give African-American workers a living wage. In a time when equal treatment was far from the norm in the South, we hired blacks in the pressing department and paid them the same wages that white people made. We had some wonderful black workers, and I still see some of their children and grandchildren around town.

At the time, my Uncle Joe was something of a misfit among the workers in the pressing room. Joe was a frustrated university professor or newspaper columnist. He could be generous, charming, and delightful—but he was not a shirt man. In those days, he was still thinking about going to New York and getting a job there. He worked in the business, but just barely—not much. Later on, Joe went to law school in Wilmington. I'm not sure if he ever took the bar.

One of Joe's jobs was that he was sort of in charge of the pressing department. The workers made up songs about everyone. So they sang, "What's wrong Joe, you got no pressers?" And they sang it in beautiful harmony. They had a song about my father and they even had one for me, something about "Freddie Boy," about the time I was in the eighth grade.

It all seems humorous now, but it wasn't then. There's nothing really humorous about a strike. The people suffered. We suffered.

There were some surprises. A short-statured woman who sewed labels—a job we found for her—became one of the most avid strikers in the group, although we had created a special machine and chair for her so her feet could reach the pedals. After the strike, she came back to work.

I'll never forget: the strike was settled the day before Pearl Harbor. Of course, it would have been settled anyway, on December 7, when America focused completely on the war.

During the war, Block made shirts for the U.S. Army. Our production was about 90 percent army shirts at that time and only 10 percent civilian shirts. We sold the government about 1,800 dozen shirts a week. At some point, someone approached my father with an offer to buy his materials from the black market during the war and make a real financial killing. He refused. When Uncle Joe came home after the war he was furious with my father for not getting into the black market. My father never even considered it. He thought it was wrong in a lot of ways. It was illegal, although most shirt factories did it. My father was patriotic and grateful.

Different army inspectors would come down and live in Wilmington and inspect the shirts. It was interesting to see. People always talk about the waste in the military, but I guarantee you the quartermasters didn't put up with a thing. They really made vendors toe the line.

Nathan Block beside the Addressograph machine in the South Third Street factory, about 1951

My father and mother were both very social and gregarious in those times. They liked to entertain and would invite soldiers to our home who would visit at the temple or the sometimes the synagogue. They would invite the men to Sunday dinner—which in those days meant the midday meal. You had breakfast, dinner, and supper. Now it's breakfast, lunch, and dinner.

Anyway, guests would come to dinner. My parents didn't get along great with all of them, but most of them they did, and they would invite them back. It was just like one big open house there, actually starting a good while before the war. Wilmington became full early on, when they army started Camp Davis, and there would be a lot of officers in town.

For some reason, my father liked to take a ride every Sunday afternoon. We'd ride around and sometimes we'd stop by somebody's house and visit. But sometimes we'd just ride around and then go back home. One particular Sunday afternoon, when we came home, there were about ten people sitting around in our back yard, just sitting there having drinks. They asked us, "Do you know what happened?"

"No," we said.

And they said, "The Japanese just bombed Pearl Harbor."

It was a very somber thing because nobody knew what was going to happen and nobody knew how bad it really was. Everybody knew it was horrible, but nobody knew right then what

Both patriotic and hospitable, Sadie Block served Sunday dinner to countless soldiers during World War II and into the early 1950s when Fred brought home friends from Camp Pickett.

we would all learn later, that 90 percent of the American fleet had been destroyed.

We sat there and talked. Then President Roosevelt gave a speech the following day and declared war on Japan and Germany. He told everyone that we would prevail. Japan had sent negotiators over to work for peace. Those men were in Washington in high-level talks while their country was bombing Pearl Harbor. It was indeed a "day that would live in infamy."

But the Jewish people in America were the first to learn about the persecution overseas. I remember the Jews who moved to Wilmington in the late 1930s. I was young then, maybe eleven years old. At Sunday School at the temple, I had seen children of the refugees who had come to Van Eeden as farmers to get away from Hitler and the Holocaust. One of the last ways out was a farming visa.

The refugee farmers were very different from Americans in obvious ways. One day I was standing on the boardwalk at Carolina Beach

Edith Wolf at Van Eeden flanked by her children, Ann and Richard—*Manfred and Ann Loeb Collection: North Carolina Collection, University of North Carolina Library at Chapel Hill*

Fred Loeb milking a cow. Dr. Johnson stood over him and instructed, "Con amore."—*Manfred and Ann Loeb Collection: North Carolina Collection, University of North Carolina Library at Chapel Hill*

Above: Ann Wolf and Fred Loeb, about 1941, as pictured in the book Van Eeden. *Left: Fred and Ann Wolf Loeb of Silver Spring, Maryland, both saved from the Holocaust by the Van Eeden project. More than fifty years after the young Fred Block avoided the European refugees, he helped seek them out—a history project that resulted in a warm friendship. (Photo by Susan Block)*

and noticed four or five kids in funny-looking hats and clothes. I hate to admit it, but it embarrassed me to be associated with them, so I just sort of shrunk into the woodwork and let them do their thing. There was one girl, a very pretty girl named Ursula, and if she had been by herself, I would probably have gone over there and spoken to her. But she was with all the rest of them.

That was over fifty years ago, and now I've gone all over the East Coast to find and talk with those same Van Eeden residents. We visited Ursula in her New York apartment, and then took six of the refugees out to dinner after becoming reacquainted with them. I'm sure at least some of the group were those same awkward-looking children I shirked on the beach that day. I'm glad I've had the opportunity, so many years later, to get to know them.

Another early rumbling of trouble in Europe reached us through a young photographer who came to Wilmington. He was also escaping Hitler, and, as far as I remember, he came from Germany. He came to our house on Chestnut Street to take family photos. His name escapes me now, but he was a big photographer in Germany. He spoke good English, but with an accent, and he had a sharp tongue. He was a very smart man. I know it took a long time to take those photos. I believe he had a Rolleiflex camera. He made sure he had everything exactly right. My mother watched every second. He went to the temple while he was here and lived near Greenfield Lake with Mr. and Mrs. Stanley Kahn. My father gave the photographer a job at the factory, but I think he moved on to a bigger city pretty quickly. Mr. and Mrs. Kahn asked him to leave after he asked them, in a commanding tone of voice, to "draw his bath" one night.

At the time, I was not proud to be Jewish, because I was different. As a child in the 1930s and 1940s, it was very difficult to be Jewish in a town like Wilmington, North Carolina. There were times when I was the only Jewish person in my class. Out of forty people in a class at Isaac Bear School, I was the only Jew. Anytime someone is the other,

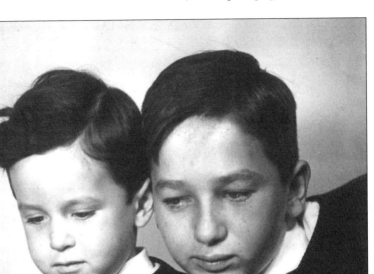

David (left) and Fred Block, photographed by Holocaust escapee Fred Wolff in 1939. Wolff lived with the Blocks briefly after fleeing Nazi Germany.

it is hard; I don't imagine it would be any easier being the only Methodist or Episcopalian in a Catholic community. I remember that every morning we had a little daily devotion in school, and it always embarrassed me a little bit because I felt left out.

Then about 1937, someone painted a swastika on the Temple of Israel building. It was the only time I ever saw fear in my father. I overheard him talking to my mother about it, and the things he said were enough to frighten me. Just imagine an unknown person painting a

Novelist Robert Ruark (1915–1965) spent most of his youth in Wilmington. In his work he later made parenthetical references to the pretty girls who worked at Block Shirts and noted that the Blocks had moved to Forest Hills Drive. In Ruark's book Poor No More, *he renamed his hometown Kensington and recorded his observations of its Jewish community: "It had never occurred to Craig that Jews were different from anybody else. In his own home town they were portion to the aristocracy of the city. That they observed the Sabbath on Saturday did not seem unusual, nor was the presence in some houses of the milchhkedikh and fleishkedikh eating utensils, one for flesh, the other for dairy products. He loved the rich Jewish food, the noodles and the matzoth and the rich desserts. The word Jew meant no more to him than the word people, or that somebody was blond or brunette. He had never heard the words Kike or Sheenie until he was exposed to the Northerners who came to Chapel Hill to take advantage of cheap tuition."*

sign of hate and death on your church. Think how frightened you would be the next time you walked through those doors. You'd wonder who was watching.

Then about 1939, the news of Jews being deported seemed to come almost daily. It was happening overseas, but who was to say at the time that it couldn't happen here? No one knew the future.

But I survived the times of embarrassment and fear. I'm very different today, and I'm proud to be Jewish. I reached one turning point in 1967, during the Six-Day War. I reached another in the past few years when I began thinking about "chosenness" and God's love for the Jews. But at the same time, I see Christianity in a better light because I know a lot more about it. I've read about the Dead Sea Scrolls. I've read about the Jewishness of Jesus and his first followers.

It's been a long learning process and I'm still in it. I keep learning. I don't know where I will be at the end of all this.

DARK CLOUDS

About the same time, my father purchased the farm in Scotts Hill for his relatives from Riga. The farm is located across the street from Poplar Grove Plantation on Highway 17. Pa bought a lot of acreage because the Blocks who were still in Riga were trying to get to America before Hitler began deporting Jews from Latvia. One group had already found refuge in Israel. I remember my Uncle Joe writing letters to Riga, back and forth. Pa put chickens, a mule, and a few pigs out there on the farm. He bought a tractor and some other equipment. The farm came with a barn to store it in.

We let a farmer live in the house to start with. But the army started building Camp Davis, the officers' training camp, about that time, and they had thousands of people working there and not enough housing for them. Pa got the idea of fixing up the house. He put running water in it and rented out rooms to the soldiers. The farmer continued to stay there and rented a room himself. And he was going to ask them to leave when his family arrived. Joe kept writing letters and receiving letters. But then one day their letters just quit coming.

Once Germany invaded Poland, we knew our relatives were gone. We knew there was no chance of them getting out. Joe kept in touch with the Blocks in Israel for years. When he finally realized they weren't coming, my father sold the farm. He should have held on to it. He was not a good businessman, outside of the factory. He said many times,

From left: Fred Block, Howard Guld, William Block, Nathan Block, and Joe Block, at the Scotts Hill farm, about 1939. (Courtesy of Cape Fear Museum)

"Put all your eggs in one basket, and watch that basket." But that's not always right.

I realized something of the gravity of the situation, but when I visited the farm, I was just a boy having fun. I rode the tractor and I enjoyed giving orders to the mule. When someone was plowing, you would tell the mule "gee" for go right and "haw" for left.

They had five hundred chickens out there. Ma Sadie went to the farm every other day to get eggs. She had many customers for the eggs. She sold wholesale to small stores like Carney's and sold retail to customers all over Forest Hills and Oleander.

Ma Sadie would tackle anything. She was that kind of person. She'd give that man hell out there at the farm. "I know you stole some of these eggs" she'd accuse him. "We don't have nearly as many eggs today as we did yesterday. Now where are the rest of these eggs?" The farmer out there was really a sharecropper. We bought the feed and everything that cost money. He did all the work. He planted the seeds, harvested the crops, and took everything to market, then kept a share of the harvest for his compensation.

I went out there a lot with Joe Block. There was only one restaurant in that area, a small one in Hampstead. You could get homemade soups and sandwiches. We would eat there and Joe would talk most of the time. He read constantly, so he could talk about almost anything. I don't think he ever noticed that he talked so much.

I don't remember my parents ever expressing their feelings about the Riga family. I'm sure they felt something, though. My father had a better sense than my mother about things like that. He would have seen the danger it could mean for everyone.

During the war, we went to look at the foreign prisoners of war who were being held in a camp at the northeast corner of Shipyard Boulevard and Carolina Beach Road. They were so young—they didn't look like the supermen they were portrayed as in all the movies. The camp was all fenced in, with high wire all around and barbed wire around the top. But at least they were alive.

TALES TOLD OUT OF SCHOOL

High school was a strange time for me because there were so many wartime things that were sad for everyone. But as a Jew, I felt even worse. Imagine if some members of a gentile family had just been exterminated because they were Christian. The Jewish religion is so old, it made me want to do something very modern in my life. I felt that way for years.

In Wilmington in the 1910s and 1920s, as I gather, a lot of men went to the poolrooms downtown, like Baxter's Pool Hall. It was the thing to do to go there and eat a sandwich and see your friends and play pool. The way I understand it, the best people in town went there. Billy Baxter owned it. He was a skinny man who always dressed in a coat and tie and spats. He was a real man about town, the way he dressed.

But for some reason billiards got to be a rough game in the 1930s and 1940s. When I went to Baxter's in the 1940s, Billy Baxter was still there—and he dressed the same way. We would go down there after school and that was sort of a hangout for us, Graham and Louis Hanson and a lot of other people. We'd shoot pool and watch the other people playing. Sometimes we'd skip school and go down and spend the day at Billy Baxter's. We'd stay off the streets, and nobody could find us there.

There was another pool room near the Atlantic Coast Line Railroad called Shepherd's, where we went sometimes. On several occasions the owner called the school and lied for us: "This is Dr. Shepherd," he'd say. "So-and-so is here and he won't be able to get to school because he's sick."

When I left high school, that was the last I saw of that. Baxter's might have been the place in the '20s. But it was on its last leg when I skipped school there. The last day of school before Christmas one year, it was snowing like crazy. I went to school and Graham didn't. He skipped that whole day. He had an old Model A Ford, and it broke down right in front of the school. The snow sort of snowed it in and it stayed there for two days.

I used to ride to school with Pa because of gas rationing and we'd go pick up Charlie and then my grandfather on the same trip. Joe was already in the army in New Guinea. Pa and Charlie would let me off at the high school and then they'd go down Princess Street to get Grandpa. Then they would go by the post office, pick up the mail, and go to work.

So one morning when I was a sophomore, I left school as soon as they dropped me off. Someone called from school and told my mother I wasn't there. She said, "I don't understand that because he left with his father and went to school." So when I got home I caught hell. When my father got home he acted like he was furious. But Ma Sadie just wouldn't stop.

Well, I thought hard about it and talked to my father. "If you'll tell her I got sick on the way to school and you took me to the doctor, I can get out of this."

Pa said, "I'm not going to lie for you."

I said, "Daddy, if you never did anything like that when you were in school, then that's fine. But if you did, I think you ought to help me."

He broke into a big smile and said he'd help—and he did.

One Friday night during my sophomore year, New Hanover was

playing Wilson in football. The game was at Wilson, nearly two hours away. I really wanted to go to that game but Ma Sadie said I couldn't. I had a date with Betty Lou Morrow that night, and she and Anne Everett were very good friends. Somehow or another I ended up with both of them on a sort of one-man double date. So we were going to a movie and we were all talking, and one of the girls suggested, "Let's drive up to the game. We can get back in time."

So I said, "That's a great idea. Let's go."

So we started driving up the road towards Wilson. I was going pretty fast somewhere between Wilmington and Paul's Place, and this truck was in front of me that I didn't see and I ran into it. It knocked the front end of the car pretty hard. I pulled off the side of the road and got out to look, and it was really bad.

I got back in the car. It started and it ran pretty well. We were creeping back to town slowly and I was thinking, "What am I going to tell my mother?"

I had wrecked the car, and cars were hard to come by back then, during the war. So we came up with the story that we'd gone to the movies but couldn't park at the movies so we parked on Water Street, which at the time was a pretty rough riverfront area with wharves and dark warehouses. My plan was for us to really go to the movies and then come out and say, "Oh my god, somebody hit the car!"

But on the way the car started smelling like it was burning up. When I hit the truck, it hit my radiator and all the water drained out. After we went in to see the movie, somebody smelled the car and called the fire department and maybe the police. They came over there and saw that it was all wrecked. Someone called my father and mother to tell them they found the car on Water Street "and it looked like foul play." And so when we came back from the movie, the car was gone.

I called the police station and told them I had parked the car on Water Street and it was gone when I came back. And they said, "You stay right there and we'll send somebody over immediately."

So there I was with two girls who were scared to death. I was hoping somebody *had* stolen the car.

The police arrived and asked me what happened, and I told them the story that we couldn't get parked anywhere but Water Street—and we went to the Carolina to see the movie.

And that's when they told me the car looked like it was burning up, and they pulled it to Macmillan Buick on Second Street and called my parents. Raymond Holland's father ran the Buick place then. When his men figured out that it was my mother's car the police said to me, "Call your Mother. She's worried to death."

And I called her and she was so happy to hear from me that she bought my story at first. I recall that my father came to get me and took the girls home. He was talking to me the whole time, saying, "You're sure you didn't wreck that car? Looks like it's been wrecked to me."

I stuck to my story and I never did tell them exactly—but I figure they knew I was lying. They couldn't break my story, and the girls never let on. But I didn't drive my mother's car for a long time after that.

I loved being out of school. My buddies and I would go down to the beach in the spring and swim, or go to the Pembroke Jones Lodge and walk around in the house. We'd sit on the nice sofas and tingle the real crystal. The abandoned lodge had one whole wing of bedrooms with bathrooms for each one. Everything made up, ready to go. Tons of beds made up.

It was just the idea of not going to school that was the attraction. We were getting away with something. Then the lodge caretaker would come and chase us away.

That's where it came in good for a teacher to like me and get me out of things.

The other thing I did sometimes I never understood. At Shandy Hall there was a guy named Hig who lived in a trailer and was crippled. The girls used to love to go there when they were skipping school. I went there maybe twice, and it gave me an eerie feeling. I just didn't like it down there.

About three weeks before graduation, I skipped school one day with Louis Hanson. We went to the beach. The following day he got called to the school office and he said he was with me. I never forgave him for that. When they called me into the office I had an excuse from my mother, which I had written myself. I could write just like her. So they pulled out all my excuses for the last six weeks and made her come to school to get me back in. They pulled them all out and made her look at all of them and see which ones she had written. Later she admitted she couldn't tell the difference. But I think they figured out I skipped eight days, so they took three points per day off my grade in every class. So that meant if I made an A, I got a D.

I made a D on everything that six weeks.

Wilmington's New Hanover High School occupies the 1300 block of Market Street. In the 1940s, it was considered one of the strongest schools academically in the state. If you had a degree from NHHS, you were already doing college-level work. (Photo from Louis T. Moore collection, New Hanover County Public Library.)

DIFFERENT DAYS

The summer between high school and college, I went to Saratoga Springs, in upstate New York, with Joe and my grandfather. I drove part of the way. We stayed overnight at a hotel in Baltimore. Joe took me to the graveyard to see where his mother was buried in Baltimore. Joe also took me to see someone in a drugstore there, one of the Hermans, my grandmother's people.

Then we went to Saratoga Springs. Joe and I spent about two days there and for some reason I can't recall, we left my grandfather there and went to New York for three or four days. Then we went back to Saratoga Springs. The hotel with the spa attached was a big frame building. I remember that I had the best lobster I had ever had in my whole life there. The chefs took it out of the shell—completely out of the shell. It was all attached, just out of the shell.

That summer after high school, in 1944, I also had my first job at the factory. I worked that summer as an assistant in the mailroom and as city delivery boy. I also helped out in the shipping department and the cutting department. It gave me a pretty good idea of what was happening in the whole factory.

That summer I also drove a city dump truck. I made more working for the city than I did working for my father. The city paid me sixty-nine cents an hour; my father paid me forty-four.

A man named Bryan Towles was involved in the paving business, and he gave me and my friends Jimmy Snow and Graham Barefoot jobs hauling asphalt to repair city streets. We had to be on the job at 7:00 a.m., and we worked for nine hours. It was exhausting, and some nights we would just stay at the Barefoots' house. Dr. and Mrs. Barefoot had four sons, Graham, Poley, Murray, and David. The boys' bedroom was a sleeping porch on the south side of their house on Forest Hills Drive. It had four windows, so each of the boys had his own window. The Barefoots always seemed to get along well. There was always a lot of laughter in that house. And I guess there was a little more because we had the house to ourselves. Dr. and Mrs. Barefoot were spending time at the farm in the country. They left Monroe, their black employee, to cook for us.

We'd get up early and Graham would drive us to work in his rumbly Model A Ford. On several occasions, the car would break down and Graham took his mother's car. I bet she was thrilled that a bunch of young men caked in asphalt were riding around in her car. My mother made me quit the job because she said she spent more money cleaning my clothes than I was making.

When I began working at the factory I saw something new about my grandfather. I knew he was generous, but I did not know the extent of his financial contributions in the name of his religion. He really believed all the things that the Bible teaches. One of those is that you never turn away anybody who comes asking for food or money—and he never did. He never turned down *anybody*.

There was a circuit of Orthodox Jews who traveled around seeking money for the cause (and I think they still do). They wore long beards and they spoke my grandfather's language. They hit him up for donations, and he never refused. He was on the list and once you got on the list . . . well, we still had people coming around in 1980 who remembered the list, and my grandfather died in 1954.

William Block gave to many rabbinical colleges, especially New Israel in Baltimore. I hope he is remembered in a generous, nice way by all who knew him. He was a very good man. He was fluent in English, German, and Yiddish. He probably spoke Russian, too, from Riga. He got the Yiddish newspaper every day. He read it to the day he died as far as I know.

It's interesting—when I was a boy my parents spoke Yiddish fluently at home. (They especially used it when discussing something they didn't want me to understand.) Then somehow it all stopped. I think the events of the 1930s frightened them out of it. But now that I am older, the words come back to me, and they are rich ones like *ganef, grossier ganef, gay shlafen, mensch, meshugeneh, putz, tsuris, zaftig.* There is nothing in English to take their place.

After my first summer of working at the factory, I spent at least some time every summer working there. I worked in the same jobs, and everybody was used to seeing me there. A lot of the employees remembered the day I was born. "Little Freddie Boy's growing up," they'd say.

Mrs. Caine, who had been in the office since 1927, gave me a four-cent raise. The office was on Greenfield Street at that time, before the extension on Third Street was built. We had a little cafeteria there that served good food—fifteen cents for a plate, plus a nickel for a drink. A woman named Bessie Beaver ran it. She was related to Alton Ketchum, who was the sewing room man, and his half-brother, Amos Carter, who was the cutting room manager.

We had a woman named Glenda Newton in the 1970s who was a pocket presser and if she wasn't there, things slowed down. She worked on a machine that was very expensive and did certain sewing maneuvers no one else could do at the time. But somehow we failed to notice when she became pregnant. One Saturday she called me and said, "Freddie, I just had a baby today."

She had just been at work the day before.

"Please don't give my job to anybody else," she said. "I'll be back on Monday."

She didn't make it to work on Monday. But she was pressing pockets again on Wednesday.

Bessie Beaver's husband, Ralph Beaver, was the night watchman. Alton and Amos had both came to work there when they were about fifteen years old. And Jesse Marshall, the office manager, had started work when he was about fifteen. I learned something from all these different people. But I especially learned from my father. The people he trusted in the community proved trustworthy to me.

Walker Taylor was a good example. Walker Taylor Insurance always had our account. The first time I met Walker Taylor III was in my father's office when I was about eighteen, and Pa had called me in because he said he had somebody he wanted me to meet. It was Walker Taylor III and his father. Walker's father had brought him out to meet my father because Walker had just gone to work with him, just as I had gone to work with my father. Going back even farther, my grandfather and his grandfather, Colonel Taylor, had had a business bond in the 1920s and 1930s.

That was the beginning of a long, pleasant business relationship. I always had the sense that Walker III was working as much for us as for his company. We trusted him completely. He had a drawer in our safe, and when he needed something, he would go over to his drawer and pull it out. He went all over that factory and kept up with every little detail. He was a real authority on safety over the years.

In a somewhat different way, my grandfather's and father's relationship with Ralph B. Williams, a successful shirt salesman for Block, paved the way for me to have a warm friendship with his son, Dr. Bertram Williams, Jr., and now, his grandson, Bert III. Those sorts of things only happen when people stay in the same business or town for a long long time.

DUTY!

I went to college early. First, my mother told a fib about my birthday and started me off in school a year early. Then my teachers pushed me through high school so that I graduated a year early. I was, by birth, supposed to be in the Class of 1946, but I graduated in 1944. After that I went to the Citadel, in Charleston, South Carolina, for one year.

I didn't want to go to the Citadel at all, but I attended for a year because of a deal I made with my father. I wanted to go to Chapel Hill—you could raise hell up there and have a good time. But I wanted a car at that time worse than anything in the world, and my father said that if I agreed to go to the Citadel for one year, it would be all right if I used Uncle Joe's car. Joe was in New Guinea at the time, fighting in the army. We made the deal when I was still a senior in high school, so I got to use the car from that time until fall semester at the Citadel, where freshmen couldn't have cars on campus.

The time to go to the Citadel came too quickly, and I found myself one sunny Sunday afternoon riding towards the train station with my mother and father. But on the way to the station, we passed some of my best friends in the back of a pickup truck—Graham Barefoot, Louis Hanson, Wimp Saleeby, and some others. They all waved goodbye to me, and it almost brought tears to my eyes.

When I got on the train, I recognized a friend, Millie Evans, who had lived on the next corner from me when we lived on Chestnut Street. I had a nice conversation with Millie and told her all my prob-

Straight lines, squared-off corners, and strictly enforced curfews made life at the Citadel a pain for Fred. "But I went to sleep every night knowing he was where he ought to be," said Sadie Block in 1999.

lems about going to the Citadel. But I've never seen her since. It happens that way.

When I got to Charleston, an officer met me at the train station and deposited me at on the Citadel campus. It so happened that Duncan Blue Black was the next person to check in. We roomed together the whole time I was at the Citadel and it was rather an odd situation because he was a junior scholastically but a freshman militarily. He had already been to college two years somewhere else.

Blue was a big man, and people were scared to tempt him too much. When they came into our room to haze us, Blue would jump up and say, "What in the hell are y'all trying to do? I'm a junior!" And it usually worked. They would back off, and we got away with murder.

I didn't like the Citadel from day one. And I liked it less and less as time went by. The main reason I didn't like it was the restrictions they put on your time. And you had to stand a certain way, eat a certain way, walk a certain way. But I figured I could put up with anything for a year, and I did. And it was just about as bad as I thought it was going to be.

In the mornings, you had to shave whether you needed it or not. You had to cut your hair once a week, whether you needed it or not. In the mornings, you had to disassemble your bed and put it in a rack until after lunch. You could lie down on it from about 1:30 until about 4:30, but then you had to put it back in the rack. It was the only time in my life I made a bed. And it had to be made properly. You had to square the corners, and it had to be made so tight a dime would bounce on it.

We had inspection every Saturday morning. The inspectors would take their white gloves and check all the places that dust would gather: over doors, beside doors. And if you had any dust, or if your shirts weren't straight, or if your underwear wasn't folded properly with a piece of paper between the folds, you would get a demerit. And if you got over four demerits you would have to walk an hour for every demerit you got over the four. And walking was up and down, up and down, in a small space. You didn't walk too many of those before you decided you didn't like that.

Your socks and shirts and underwear had to have that piece of paper in the center and none of the edges of the fabric could show. Blue and I didn't want to fold those things all the time and put a piece of paper into each piece of clothing. So we just set up some underwear in our drawers for inspection and left them there the whole year, while we stashed the clothes we really wore somewhere else.

Even though the room was tiny, we got along very, very well the whole year. We kept in touch after that every now and then. The last time I saw Blue was when he came to Wilmington about 1995. Since then he has passed away.

In high school, it was easy to go to the infirmary and get out of class for a day. They would send you home, but we didn't go home. So I thought I could get out of class at the Citadel. We had an old geezer, a retired army officer named Colonel Cathcart, in charge of sick bay. His wouldn't let you get away with anything. He got gassed or something in service and spoke sort of funny. So when I went to sick bay I tried the same thing as in high school, but he looked me over carefully and said, "Duty!" in his own low gravelly voice.

I had a 102-degree temperature one day and I thought for sure I'd get out of class *that* day. But once again, just the word, "*Duty!*" I never tried him again unless I was really sick.

The only time I actually got out of class was when I was playing touch football and I got completely knocked out. He kept me overnight in the infirmary and the next day he let me stay out of class. So looking back, I guess he *was* a pretty good doctor.

There were some pleasant moments at the Citadel. One was when I had Betty Lou Morrow come down for a dance. It was a grand dance. They ought to do something to make you happy down there. They opened up barracks that were not in use for the girls. The dance was over at twelve o'clock, and of course, in keeping with everything else at the Citadel, we had to be in by one a.m. The mess hall fixed a very nice breakfast the next morning for us guys and our dates. Then I put Betty Lou on the bus at five that afternoon to go home.

Beginning with the last hundred days of the school year, I used to keep a record of how many days, and how many hours, and how many minutes I had left at the Citadel. I filled up a whole page with calculations, then I would fill up another page. I worked on it every day. Gas was tight then, and in the interest of speed, as soon as I got out I hitchhiked home.

A BLOCK IN BLUE HEAVEN

After my horrible year in Charleston, I came home and met up in Wilmington with several of my Citadel friends—Ted Carroll, Ted Crozier, and Bill Wells. The two Teds were from Washington, and Bill was from Elm City.

We spent a very nice week together at Wrightsville Beach. They were staying at the Carolina Yacht Club, and I stayed out there with them a few nights. After that, my mother really had hopes that I would return to the Citadel because I "enjoyed my friends so much," she said. But there was no way I was going back—not for any amount of money or cars.

Ted Carroll finally talked me into going to Chapel Hill, because that was where he was headed. So I started classes that summer. At that time, practically all the dormitories were taken up by the Navy ROTC. Ted and I started looking for a room, and the closest one we could find was on Cameron Avenue. Mrs. Delancey owned the house. There were four rooms upstairs and she rented all four of them out.

And strange as it seems, two of the boarders were guys from Wilmington that I didn't know before, Jimmy Simpkins and Donald Mathews. Donald's father had a candy company; I think it was the same one that used to be on Hanover Street, where the Block factory later moved. We became pretty good friends after that and went out to dinner a number of times when I was there. Chapel Hill was very differ-

Father and son Nathan (left) and Fred Block get ready to take in a college football game, about 1946.

ent from the Citadel. We drank beer most every night and did a little bit of studying. The Sigma Nu house was next door to Mrs. Delancey's, and I ate my meals there. The Sigma Nus were a wild bunch. They used to take wooden chairs and ride down the steps on them.

A couple of friends from Wilmington drove up to visit me one night in a Model A Ford. We decided to go out to a nightclub that evening, the only one in Chapel Hill. It was out on the way to Greensboro, past Carrboro. It was pretty empty when we got there, so we decided to go back to town to get dates. I rounded up several girls and we headed back to the club.

On the way back, riding down the wrong side of the street, the driver of our car ran head-on into a motorcycle coming the other way. The poor guy turned a flip in the air and I really thought at first he was dead, the way he lay there. The police came and we all got out of the car. Of course, they started questioning all of us—what we were doing, where we were going. Being as how my friend was driving, they put him in jail. Then they started asking each one of us, separately, different questions. They asked me where the whisky was and I said, "In the car."

The police looked in our car and didn't see any whisky. They came back to me and asked again, "Where is the whisky?"

"It's in the car," I said.

"Well, we didn't find it. Show us."

So I went and got the whisky—from the police car, not ours. When they called me out of the car to ask me questions, I had it with me because I had helped pay for it and it was our whisky. So I was sitting there in the police car with the whisky!

At the police station I was interrogated again. After several hours of going back and forth, I called my buddy's mother in Wilmington and told her what happened. Somehow she got a lawyer and got him out of jail, then came the next morning to take him home. It was a very scary night for me—and a truly sobering lesson.

While in Chapel Hill, we all used to meet every afternoon at the bar right next to the theater, on the side of Franklin Street toward campus. After we were pleasantly tight, we would go to dinner. We usually ate at the Porthole, Ptomaine Tommy's, or the Rathskeller. One night after drinking a little more than usual, I came home after hours and, as to get back in I climbed the fire escape that went straight to my room. But that night I slipped and fell all the way to the ground. Amazingly, I wasn't hurt at all. I was quite relaxed.

Because of the war, there wasn't too much going on in Chapel Hill on the weekends. Most of the students were Navy ROTC, and they didn't get out much. So about half the time we came home to Wilmington. Arthur Bluethenthal had just gotten out of the army and he had a big Buick convertible, and I would ride home with him.

After two semesters, I just wasn't doing too well with grades in Chapel Hill. So I quit and came back home to work, but I have never lost my love for Chapel Hill.

GEORGIA FROLIC

During the Christmas season of 1945, I ran into an acquaintance who was older than me named Truman McGill, and we started taking about what I was going to do now that I had left Chapel Hill. Truman went to the University of Georgia, he said, "and that's a better party school than Chapel Hill."

About that time, I made a snap decision that I'd go to the University of Georgia too. I packed my suitcase and got on the train that night to Hamlet, where I changed trains and went to Athens, Georgia. So there I was at six in the morning all by myself. I went to the hotel in Athens, but there were no rooms at that inn. I started talking to the room clerk, who was a student at the university. He said I could go sleep on the sofa if I wanted to, or I could go in the kitchen and make myself some breakfast. So I went in the kitchen and made bacon and eggs, and sat down in the kitchen to eat. I asked him how I could get into the university and he said to me, "You don't have any transcripts or anything?"

And I said, "No, I just decided to go to the university."

He said, "There's a Miss Montgomery in the admissions office. Ask for her and tell her you know me. She'll either throw you out or be nice to you."

But she turned out to be very nice. I told her what courses I had had and she accepted them somehow or another. I guess she confirmed

Fred Block's University of Georgia student ID photo and student athletics ticket, 1946–47

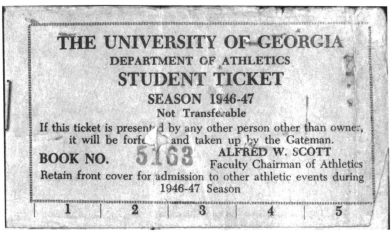

them later on, but I never heard from her again. So there I was, enrolled as a student at the University of Georgia.

There was sort of a lull between semesters. I had about three days before classes started. I decided to go back to Chapel Hill for a few days. I took the train to Raleigh, but I found out I didn't have enough money to get all the way there. So I got the train to Hamlet and instead of getting off at Hamlet like I was supposed to, I hid in the bathroom and stayed on the train to Raleigh. From there I hitchhiked to Chapel Hill. I went back to my old room, and my half hadn't been rented yet. I spent two nights with Ted Carroll before we went back to Athens.

I had been in a joint room, a sort of school ward, with about twenty people. When I got back my bags had been moved to a nice dormitory named Clark-Howell. They set me up in a corner room, right next to the football stadium and across the street from the fairgrounds.

After I was down in Athens for about a week, I wanted to see what Atlanta looked like. So I hitchhiked to Atlanta and when I got there, I found out I didn't have much money—maybe two dollars. I went to a store and tried to cash a check, only to find out that they didn't cash out-of-town checks, particularly for strangers. Next I went to a bank, thinking they would cash a check. No again.

What was I going to do? I talked to a very nice lady at the bank and told her I just had to cash a check. So she thought a minute and said, "Do you know anybody in your bank in Wilmington?"

I thought a minute and said, "I know the president and his secretary." The president was Goodlett Thornton at Wilmington Savings and Trust Company. The secretary, Mary Graham, had been my kindergarten teacher at St. James Church. So I called long distance, identified myself, and asked for Miss Graham, except by that time I think she was Mrs. Shigley. She came on the line and said, "Is that you, Freddie?"

"Yes it is," I said. "But I need you to tell these people that it is really me."

So she asked me, "Do you remember coming to my house for lunch, and do you remember what we did after lunch?

"Yes I do," I answered. "We played tennis."

She was married to someone who was an official at the Dow Chemical Company. They had a little compound right there near the Dow plant. There were only about four or five houses where they lived, but they had a private tennis court.

So she said, "Well you've got to be Freddie, 'cause you are the only one who would know that."

So I thanked her and she got on the phone with the clerk at the bank and said she could cash the check for any amount she wanted to. Then I had money in my pocket and was very happy when I returned to Athens.

That next day on campus, I ran into Margaret Wenberg and Barbara Leeuwenburg from Wilmington. It gave me somebody that I knew in the school. I went down there not knowing if there would be anyone else from home. I used to have lunch with them maybe once or twice a week, usually at the Varsity. Athens had its own Varsity restaurant. It was much smaller than the one in Atlanta, but the food was the same. It was directly across the street from the center of campus. I ate a lot back then, but I burned it up.

I met Barbara's boyfriend, Norman Carnes, from Athens, and we became very close friends. He was the only person I really got close to down there that I considered a good friend. I spent the night at his par-

Nathan Block in his office at Southland, 1952

ents' home several times when I would go back to visit. He was killed in the Korean War only a few years afterward—and thinking about that makes me sad all over again.

After a while in Georgia, I came home between quarters. I was sitting around the house one night and my father said, "You're not working very hard at school. Why don't you quit school, go on the road, and make some money?"

That was on a Wednesday. So Thursday morning I started out "on the road" as the new Block salesman for eastern North Carolina and all of Virginia. It had been Moe Guld's job, before he and Aunt Esther had moved to Wilmington.

Before I left that morning, I asked my father, "What do I say about the shirts? What do I answer when they ask me about the thread count, or some other technical question?"

So he said, "Well, just tell them you've got nice shirts."

FOUR-WHEEL SCHOOL

I went to work for my father in earnest in the fall of 1945. The big thing in those days was the Cantfade, a feature my father based on another company's shirt, the Nofade. At the time, having something that did not fade was a big deal. But he figured out how to keep colors from fading and called it Block's Cantfade Shirt. There is a lot of copying that goes on in the shirt world. It's just part of the business, part of the competition. The thing about my father was that he could figure things out.

When I went to work, I tried to help out a friend from Chapel Hill, Julian Highsmith, who was selling what amounted to an early version of Muzak. We installed it in the factory and started playing music in the lunchroom and during the ten-minute morning and afternoon breaks. I started out by playing it on the factory floor, but that just didn't work out. There was too much noise for people to hear it. All those sewing machines. In those days, though, I never minded noise. The deafening sound of sewing machines meant money in the bank.

The first trip I ever took as a traveling salesman was by bus. I had a suitcase and a sample case—and I had to carry both of them everywhere. It sort of weighed me down, but I made it all right.

After that first two-week trip, I bought a car. It was a 1944 Chevrolet two-door sedan. It cost $1,425. After that, I didn't have to

A window display featuring the Cantfade label. These mock displays served as a selling tools for stores across the country.

tote two suitcases everywhere.

I enjoyed the driving. I put fifty thousand miles on my car that first year. Every time I passed by the crabmeat place north of Richmond, Virginia, I'd stop and get a pound of backfin or lump crabmeat and eat it while I was driving. I'd listen to the radio and some of the programs. There were very few four-lane roads back then, and I was pretty good at passing cars on the two-lane roads. To keep on schedule, you had to pass a lot of cars.

Soon after I started selling, Phil Shulman, Shirley Block's first husband, tried to help me. He said, "One of my best friends runs this store"—a big department store on Church Street in Norfolk. Phil called the boss ahead of time and basically asked him to go over the buyer's head and tell him to buy from me.

So I told Phil, "Thank you!" And I went to call on them, and the

Southland promotional card

buyer came out and I told him who I was.

"I'm from Block Shirts," I said. I laid the shirts out. And I said, "And I really think they're nice shirts."

And the buyer said, "Well, my boss thinks they're nice, too. So if he thinks they're nice and you think they are nice, then go over there and sell them to him." And I was really taken aback. This man was really a strong buyer, and he didn't take any guff from anybody.

So he told the boss, "If you want to buy shirts from him, you buy them. But I'm not going to buy them. And if you want to fire me for that, that's alright—fire me."

I learned that day that you never go over anybody's head if you can help it. So just in that short period of time, I learned a good lesson. I kept learning lessons the whole time I was traveling.

I went on to Richmond after that. I still hadn't learned to pay enough attention to my wallet, and I ran out of money again. So I asked one of the customers if he'd cash a check for me.

And he said, "No. I don't know you. You say you're Fred Block, from Block Shirts, but I've never met you before. I just don't cash checks for strangers."

I went down to a bank and they wouldn't cash my check either. So

I'm sitting there with money in the bank, but nobody would cash my check. I called my father and asked him to wire me some money. And he did. He understood that people don't cash checks along the road.

I learned another lesson that first month or two—or maybe there's no lesson, but just a cute story. I walked into a store and the buyer said, "Where's your hat?"

"I don't wear hats," I said. "I just don't like hats and they don't feel good on my head."

He said, "Well, I sell hats, and unless you wear a hat, I'm not going to buy shirts from you."

I said, "Okay, thank you very much." And I walked out.

Now, fast-forward about two years, and I saw the same man at a party in Richmond. And he came over to me and asked, "Where have you been? I've been looking for you for about two years, to buy shirts from you."

I said, "Well, remember you told me you wouldn't buy shirts from me because I wouldn't wear a hat."

"Oh, I was just kidding," he said. "I didn't really mean that. I didn't need shirts that day. I didn't mean not to come back. Please come back." And I went back, and he ended up being one of the best customers I ever had.

One customer in particular made me think hard about people's pride in their choices. In a store in Elizabeth City, North Carolina, I saw a competitor's shirt that was much overpriced. So I told the man, "See that shirt there. It's way overpriced. My shirts are a lot better than that shirt and more reasonable."

So the merchant proceeded to tell me that he did not want to hear that his shirts were overpriced and not fine. "I bought that shirt," he said. "And I thought it was a good shirt. So when you tell me it's over-priced, you are telling me that I don't know how to buy."

I asked him, "What should I say? I believe what I said."

He answered, "Just don't say anything about a buyer's current

Fred Block, Betty Lou Morrow, Ann Everett, and John Burney, about 1945, with props in a Carolina Beach photo booth

choice." And he was right.

I did learn a lot as a traveling salesman. In my way of thinking, everybody should start out in life in sales, selling some sort of a commodity that people need: shirts, ladies' dresses, underwear. Anything that people really need.

After I became a traveling salesman, I spent some time with Graham Barefoot at old Wake Forest. My friend Beverly Barge lived at the fraternity house across the hall from Graham, but he went home to Durham on the weekends, so I used his room then. My girlfriend at the time, Betty Walters, had to be in at eleven on Friday night, so after I dropped her off I would go back to the fraternity house and pick up Graham. Then we'd go to the Wake Forest Tearoom and sit down and drink beer and solve all the world's problems.

When we couldn't hold any more beer we'd go to downtown Wake Forest to Shortie's, the only thing open. It was a redneck all-night cafe. Farmers patronized it, and the jukebox didn't have anything but hill-billy music. We'd order breakfast, but we were the only college boys there. They didn't like us very much. Our favorite song on the jukebox was "When They Baptized Sister Lucy Lee." We must have played it ten times every night we were there, and Graham would sing with it. They'd beg us to quit.

John Burney was at Wake Forest Law School at the same time. I had known him in Wilmington, but not very well. He was Graham's cousin and he lived a few blocks from our house on Chestnut Street. At Wake, he was already married. John and his wife, Betty, were living in an apartment. He started selling shirts for me and he made a lot of money doing it. That was the time when we became good friends. Today I count Graham and John my best friends.

About that time I got my first large boat. And by large, I mean something over twenty-five feet. I called the boat the *Cantfade*. When I bought the boat, my father said anybody that would get up at six in the morning to go fishing was crazy. So the first morning David and I were ready to go out fish-

The Cantfade Christmas party, about 1948, was held in the Armory—now the Cape Fear Museum building. Jesse Marshall (back, at left) was a longtime comptroller at Block; his wife, Dorothy, was a groundbreaking staff member at UNCW. Joe Maultsby (with cigarette) was a fabric cutter. Jack Lowrimore (left foreground, next to Fred) was a friend of Fred's.

ing, my father sort of sheepishly said, "I think I'll go with you." So we all went out about six in the morning and caught about four or five fish. We brought them home and ate those fresh fish, and my father was the one who was hooked. After that, he hardly ever missed a chance to get up early to fish. We kept that boat for a while. And then, after several years without a boat, David and I bought the *Ma Sadie*. Our mother never liked the name of the *Cantfade*, so I was sure to name the next one after her.

While I was a traveling salesman, I was home for the weekend and Jimmy Shipp of Dan River Mills was in town selling cloth to my father and Joe. So I went down to the factory to help them pick out fabrics. As the morning wore on, we decided that we had done enough work and we wanted to see a new thing in town: the Azalea Festival. The parade route at that time was right down Front Street. It started at the Atlantic Coast Line Railroad offices and went south on Front Street.

So we grabbed two bottles of liquor and rode down to the Wilmington Hotel. Our rooms faced Front Street and were on the third floor, so we had ringside seats. We proceeded to order some chasers and watch the parade. We had a blast. The only thing I remember about the parade was that the floats were pulled by tractors, and some of the tractors had flowers on them. The Wilmington Hotel had a very nice dining room, so we all ate lunch after the parade.

The Cantfade *in the Inland Waterway, about 1949. In the background, Faircloth's Restaurant sits next to the old Wrightsville Beach bridge.*

MORE DUTY

So, after I traveled for maybe three years, the Korean War came up. I didn't have any desire to serve in the Korean War. I went down to the draft board and I said, "Well, what's going to happen? Are y'all drafting people?"

And they said, "Oh yeah, we're drafting, but you don't have to worry. You're way down the list. You can decide what service you want to go into. Go ahead—you've got plenty of time."

The next day, I got a letter in the mail. "You have been selected. Report at such and such a time . . . " And I went down to the draft board and I was livid. I said, "I was just down here yesterday and you told me not to worry."

And they said, "We got orders to draft so many people. I'm sorry, but you're one of the ones we had to draft." So I was drafted into the United States Army for twenty-one months. I finally got out of the Citadel—and then there I was in the army.

It ended up being two years, minus three weeks. I reported for training at Camp Pickett, Virginia in September 1950. In 1951, the army sent me to Germany. It took ten days to sail over there and ten days back. The troop ship we went over on was the USS *Gen. M. L. Hersey*. On the way over, on the last day, we were in the river steaming into Bremerhaven and we saw a ship about the same size as ours coming towards us.

Above: Fred Block snapped this photo on November 4, 1952, from the deck of the Hersey *just before the* Maipu *sank. Below: Certificate from the* General Hersey, *the vessel on which Block was sailing when it collided with the* Maipu.

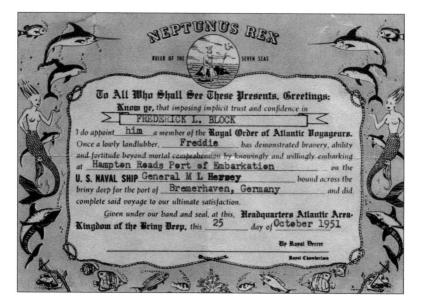

It was a foggy morning, just before breakfast, and you could hear the foghorns. Suddenly we struck the other ship: *Bam!* Luckily the other vessel was empty, except for the crew. It was a new Argentine cruise ship, the *Maipu*, and had just let off all its passengers. The crew were deadheading somewhere to pick up another load. Nobody got hurt, but it was scary. You could see the bow of our ship all busted in. I had a camera in my berth and took a photo of the ship on that foggy morning. Everybody on the *Maipu* got off in lifeboats. If they had hit us, I'm sure our ship would have sunk. After we saw that everyone got off safely, I went up to the mess hall and had breakfast.

When I went into the army, my grandfather was still vibrant and active. He could speak German fluently, so while I was in Germany I got some of my girlfriends to write him letters. I was disap-

Fred Block on leave, French Riviera, 1952

pointed when he never answered any of them. I thought he would get a kick out of exchanging letters in German.

When I came back, I found out why. He had lost his capacity to do things like that. He didn't know I had written him those letters. He didn't even know me. It was very sad.

In Germany, we marched a lot. We worked up to a twenty-five-mile hike. We walked every Wednesday afternoon. I had a friend who always told me to keep him going straight because he was going to sleep. I tried it but never did do it.

It started getting cold over there about my birthday, November 17. Real cold. It snowed about then too, and the snow stayed on the ground. It was about four feet deep until spring. And when it started melting, you couldn't go outside for about a week because you would

Skeets Majeski (left) and "Bud," both soldiers from Stamford, Connecticut, who served with Fred (center) at Camp Pickett in 1951, enjoyed lots of Southern hospitality when they visited the Blocks.

sink up to your waist in mud. I made up my mind that if I had a choice, I'd never be cold again.

I used to go out after the hikes. I'd go out at night and drink beer. I made up my mind the army wasn't going to break me, no matter what they would do. No one else in our company went out after the long hikes, ten miles or more.

I had only one long leave during my time in Germany, and I went to France with Phillip Overbaeur. We went to Paris, the French Riviera, and the Italian Riviera, and then came back. We had a great time and I met some real characters.

I had been working for three years before I went into the army so I had some money when I was in Germany. I paid the taxi driver to be on call for me the whole time I was off duty. When I got through on Saturday afternoon, he was there waiting for me. Wherever I went, he would be outside waiting.

I had two years of experiences in the army—lots of good, bad, and indifferent things happened. But I learned there, too. I learned a lot in the army, and I think anybody who's ever been in the military learns a lot. And when I came home I knew I had done my duty to God and my country.

While I was in the army, a salesman named Irv Sims took over my territory. Then Howard Guld took over from him, and he was still working there when his father, Moe, died. Moe Guld had quit selling that territory when World War II started because shirt sales stopped. About halfway through the war, my father decided to open up another factory because we didn't have enough production to meet the demand for army shirts, and Benson, North Carolina, looked like a good location for it.

So he put Moe up in Benson as the plant manager. Moe did a good job there. He was a good people manager and the people loved him. He had a good, smart woman behind him, too. My Aunt Esther had a quick business mind. I'm sure she gave him the right kind of feedback.

There was a lady who owned a boarding house and served meals, and we ate there when we visited. It was good food—country food served boarding-house style. Her husband was an insurance salesman. She had one of these old-timey beds, high off the floor, with a canopy over the top of it. But she wouldn't sell that bed. I was there when an attorney tried to buy it, and she said she got lots of offers but she wasn't selling.

When Moe Guld died, Howard took over the his father's job in Benson.

I was finally released in September of 1952, and when I came home my mother and father were obviously very happy to see me. And I told them I was going to take six months off. "Don't even talk about me going back to work right now," I said. "When I was in the army, I couldn't do what I wanted to do. Six months is not too much to ask. I've got enough money that I saved up before I went in the army. And I just want to see Dick Dunlea and Graham and Jere Freeman and all my old friends—then have some time to bum around the country and do what I want to do."

"Oh, no problem. You can do that," they told me.

BACK TO WORK

The first day or two I was home I just lounged around the house. And then the next day my father said, "There's going to be a shirt show in Florida and we can go and help the salesmen. You'll have plenty of time to rest in the sun."

That sounded pretty good. I had had a headache ever since I got out of the army, but when we got on the plane, for some unknown reason, my headache went away. When we got to Florida we sold lots of shirts and we had a good time. Then we came home and I said, "Okay, now I'm going to take some time off."

And he said, "Okay."

The next day Pa woke me up again. He got me up and conned me into going to work full-time, and I never got my little vacation. He told me, "A man I had working named John Wallace left two weeks ago to go to work for another company and I could really use you."

I reminded him that I didn't want to go to work right then. I wanted to travel around the country a little bit.

So he said, "Well, just come in for a few days. You don't even have to come in as early as I do. I'll get up and go in early and you come in a little later. It's fine." I took it in good faith.

The next day he went in early and I came in later. The next morning, he got up and woke me up. Then my mother said, "Please, darling. Just come in here and eat some breakfast, darling. If you'll come eat breakfast right now, it will help me so much. Then I can get all the dishes off the table. You'll enjoy being with your father."

So I got up and ate breakfast, and somehow or another he coerced me into going to work that early.

That was in 1952. I worked from 1952 until 1986, and I hardly missed a day. And I usually worked a long day.

But I learned a lot. In fact, whenever I asked my father for a raise, his standard reply was, "It's not important how much money you make, it's only important that you learn the business. If you learn the business, nobody can take that away from you."

And you know, he was right. I still wanted more money and thought I needed more money. My father was not generous with salaries because he thought the money should stay in the company, with the family as stockholders. It was that same old theme of his: "Put all your eggs in one basket and watch that basket."

But if you learn the business, whatever business, nobody can take that business away from you. You know that business.

That first day, my father took me over to John Wallace's former desk, which was piled high. John, who took a job out of town but years later would return to work at Block, was sort of an assistant to my father. It was a big job. It was second command. My father showed me what needed to be done and it was easy for me because I had been around the factory so long that I had it caught up in three days.

So my father hooked me good. I only had about a three- or four-day vacation. But it made me feel pretty good, for him to think that I could do John's job. And I had money coming in and I had plenty of money from when I was a salesman—and when you've got money and you're single and twenty-three years old, you're in good shape. So I was having a good time and I was learning the business.

That was a time when we were doing gangbusters. Right after World War II, there was a recession, but by 1953, things were good. We were selling every shirt we could make. I was in charge of produc-

Simple and bare, Fred Block's new office was powered by human energy.

tion. I kept pushing for more production and pushing and pushing.

At first I had a desk in the corner of my father's office. I was very unhappy with my desk and sharing an office with him. So I built a little office, just as you came into the factory. I moved the payroll from an office that was too crowded, the main office on Third Street. I built a small office plus a sort of reception room where we put the time clocks, and I had my office there too. It was a small private office, with the two payroll girls.

Moving the office took about a year. I was by myself down there. I was gradually taking over things as I learned how to do the different jobs. My father wasn't lazy by any means, but he was ready to step away from some of the work.

The new offices made things flow better. People had the payroll office right there at the plant. I put it at the corner of the ell because I could use walls that were already there in the construction—I always had to justify costs to my father.

After the first shirt show I went to in Florida, I went every year. My father never went again. Even though he was a great shirt man, he didn't like shows. But it did me a lot of good, because I could do things for the shirts that made them sell better. I would put different things in the collars to make the shirts look fresher, so that they wouldn't get busted down by handling. I would fold them better. I learned lots of little things that really helped the shirts. You don't know that unless you're on the selling end.

For a lot of years, I was really learning. But I was always very ambitious to do things better—to open a new factory, or make a better shirt, or to take on as many jobs as I could. I learned things that worked, like telegrams. I remembered that one great thing about weddings and bar mitzvahs when I was a child was the reading of telegrams from well-wishers. So I thought they might be dramatic enough to get payments from slow customers. It worked. Telegrams embarrassed people into paying their bills.

When I started in the business, all the stockholders had to personally sign notes at the bank to borrow money. At the time, the stockholders were my grandfather, my father, Charlie, Joe, and Esther. After I was in the business for a few years and understood that we had a very strong company financially, I didn't see any reason to personally sign notes. So after negotiating for six months or so, I persuaded the bank to do away with that practice. Then any of the officers could go down and sign for the corporation. In the old days, if there was a default they could have gone after one or all of those who signed the loan.

Shep Salzman worked for my father. He was a good man and my father wouldn't promote him like he thought he should be promoted, so he went to South Carolina and opened a shirt factory called Wings that sold more shirts than Block at one time. They were a semi-advertised brand, and they did very well. My father never expressed regret, but he was wrong not to promote Shep.

At first, Pa took care of buying the cloth in New York. Every now and then, he took salesman Abie Ruben with him. Abie was the one who couldn't say his v's. He called a vent a "went." That little flaw helped him sell many a shirt. He was charming—and always immaculately dressed. Abie was better known around town for being part owner of the Plantation Club out on the Carolina Beach Road in the 1940s and 1950s. He tried to make it a real New York restaurant, but not enough people in Wilmington were willing to pay the prices.

But Abie was a full-time salesman, and he really knew what buyers were looking for. He was good to have along in New York so he could tell my father what shirts would be a success. Pa was very frugal and only bought exactly what he thought would sell. He did a good job of it, but it was stressful for him to run the factory in Wilmington and take all those buying trips to New York. Block was supplying shirts to 2,000 outlets across the country at the time. During World War II, his stress dropped to nothing, even though the factory made a million shirts. But he only had one customer to please: the U.S. Government. He was so relaxed he got fat.

Then after the war, things were more complicated again, and fabric was hard to come by. Joe was fresh back from the service, and my father sent him to New York to buy. Joe could be very charming and could talk to people anywhere about almost anything. He managed to make friends with some of the key mill people in New York. He made deals and did all sorts of things to get the cloth. All fabric was at a premium, but especially white. White shirts were like gold right after the war, and they still were when I first became a traveling salesman in 1947.

At first Joe did a good job of buying. But over time, that changed. He would go out with the fabric representatives and they would wine and dine him. Then he would buy lots of cloth and he would never sign an order form. One day a truck would back up to the factory in Wilmington and unload twenty cases of cloth, and I wouldn't know what it was or where it came from. One time he bought blue when he was supposed to buy green. I'd call New York and they'd say, "Oh, Joe bought that."

And I'd say, "This is not in the line, and half of it we don't need and I already have cloth in the warehouse."

Joe Block and his date, Irene, New York City, 1954

But Joe continued to go out with the people in New York and have two or three martinis—and he'd always buy. The only way I stopped that was I told the New York office I was not going to receive anything unless I had papers beforehand. After that, the cloth people had to contact me first and could not ship until I approved everything. And that's when Joe got mad with me.

Joe was something—but he was not a shirt man. I don't know why my father let him get by with all that. He would just say, "They are my family." Though my father ran the factory, he made sure his brothers had equal ownership, dignity, and respect.

My father was very indulgent with Joe. And Joe didn't venture far into circles where he wasn't indulged. He got to know two sisters once who were quite attractive. They had some connection to the Rosenberg jewelry people that Ma Sadie knew. The girls lived in New York, and he took both of them out occasionally. I think it was nothing but flirtation, but one day one of the sisters showed up in Wilmington and knocked on his door. She said she wanted to marry Joe. *Marry Joe?* He disappeared out the back door and didn't come home until she went back to New York. That was the last we heard about that. No wife would have put up with Joe the way my father did. I must say my mother saw through Joe and saw a lot of the family's problems before my father did.

When Hurricane Hazel arrived in October 1954, I went to work like any other morning. We had warning that there might be a bad hurricane coming, but I did not think it would hit us like it did. When I got to work, weather conditions changed quickly. Water started rising from the Cape Fear River up the street towards Second Street. It was really scary. The only people remaining in the businesses down there were the executives. Everybody else was scared, so they went home. Finally we all decided we were better off going home.

After the storm moved through and the wind died down, I got up with my father and David and we went down to Wrightsville Beach to see what was happening. When we got there, we found boats scattered across the highway, all the way down. We went to check on the *Cant-fade* at Wrightsville Marina. We had tripled-tied it before the hurricane. There was only a single line left in place.

Jere Freeman was living at Wrightsville Beach at the time, and he couldn't get on the beach for two days. They didn't let anybody on because of the washed-out roads. The Carolina Yacht Club was really beat up. My friends who were members said they were going to build it back like it was. But other than that, there wasn't that much damage for the people I knew. The factory was fine, and fortunately there were no catastrophes involving the employees as far as we could tell.

SOUTHLAND

In the 1960s I took on an increasing responsibility for the business. For decades, my father had the first parking spot at the factory. Charlie had the second, and I had the third. In 1969, my father and Charlie retired and I became CEO. I enjoyed pulling into that first parking spot.

I don't know that I worked any harder after they left. I had actually run the company for three years. My father was satisfied with the results. But I wasn't working to impress him. It came naturally. It never even occurred to me to slack off. I just put hard work—effective hard work—on a pedestal. I worked hard all day, sometimes returned to the office after supper, and woke up during the night thinking about problems and solutions.

About 1960, I solved one of the biggest sales dilemmas the company had faced. Of the Block sales force, I was the one who finally sold shirts to Belks—one of the most important department store chains in the Southeast. I first noticed the problem back when I was a traveling salesman. I'd always call on several stores. I would sell some. The individual stores always liked our shirts, but the Belk corporate buying office didn't purchase them. As the years went by it was more and more annoying for me, and I wanted to do something about it.

The Belk problem was a prime example of family business at its worst. At the time, Joe Block was salesman for Belks and Efird's, both

Above: Southland factory workers line up for Fourth of July party, 1966. Below: Longtime presser Lucille Tyson (right), 1966. (Courtesy Lower Cape Fear Historical Society)

Block cutter Henry Croom, 1966 (Courtesy Lower Cape Fear Historical Society)

of whose offices were in Charlotte. My father should have taken the account away from him years ago—but instead he indulged him as usual. Joe would sell only a few to each, more to Efird's than to Belks. After watching the situation for years, I decided that if Joe couldn't sell Belks, I would sell them myself. I went up there and they said, "Thank you but we've already bought for the season."

So the next year, I went up when our line was ready. I took fifteen cases of shirts and took a young man to assist me. He kept bringing them in and out. I showed Walter Reid, the buyer, all I had. His boss was Ralph Klemmer, the men's merchandise manager for the buying service. They both told me how wonderful Joe was. "He's the nicest guy," they said.

It was very odd. Ralph and Walter said Joe always thanked them for not buying. They *never* bought, but he continued to visit them and always said "Thank you." They always wondered why, but never said anything about it to his face.

So when I got through with my Belks presentation, Walter said, "Thank you, but we've already bought."

And I said, "Wait a minute. When do you buy?"

And he said, "Didn't you know—we always buy two months earlier than this."

So the next time, I went early and took fewer shirts. Walter bought some to try.

Then the next time I went up for the new season, I said, "Walter, if you don't buy I'll never come back because I've brought you some very nice things that are *just right* for Belks and I made them up ahead of our usual schedule."

He said, "Now don't take that attitude," and we struck up a very nice friendship that is still dear to me today. They had a little booklet that they put their shirts in, and Walter showed me how to put our shirts in there—and we got the shirts and samples to him. When their orders came in they had bought about 3,000 dozen, instead of 700 or

800 dozen. He said, "You mean you didn't back me up? How will we make up the overage?"

I said, "Give me some leeway, I'll fill the order as best I can." We had some surpluses that were close, and I substituted them and everything worked out.

So from then on, it was smooth sailing with Belks. They were very fair in everything they did. And Joe never forgave me.

So one day, Walter asked us if we had any flannel shirts. I sent him some, and after that he sold 3,000 to 5,000 dozen a season. Some years you sold a lot of flannel, some less. Plaid shirts were about as stable as anything there was. And Oxford shirts—we always had those. So Belks

Nathan (left) and Fred Block, about 1977

became our biggest customer. It was by far the largest customer Block ever had. We used to make 10,000 dozen shirts just for their Founders' Day Sale every year.

After several years of working together, Walter and I figured out that the best thing for us to do was to meet in New York. There were about twenty companies there that sold cloth, and we would get all their line in the New York office over a weekend and go over them and see what Walter wanted to buy for the next season. We'd make up sample shirts from all the materials, and he would pick out what he actually wanted to buy. He would usually buy between 10,000 and 12,000 dozen to start off the season.

Mr. Klemmer said, "Yankees come down here and think we think

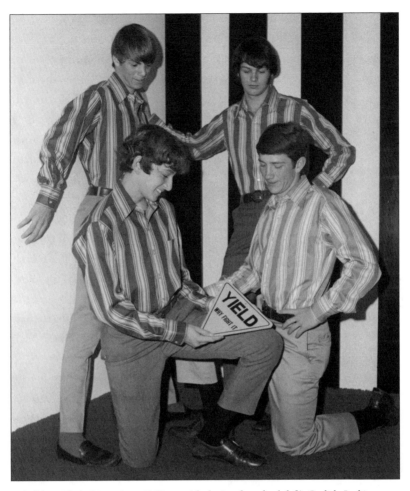

Modeling Block shirts, circa 1969, are (clockwise, from back left) Carlisle Jenkins, Henry Nunalee, Kevin Dineen, and Billy Block.

slow because we talk slow, and they think they're smarter than we are, but they usually find out they're wrong."

Belks was important to us, but there were always other things going on.

One routine form of shirt sale went unannounced. We always sold a lot of shirts to funeral homes. They didn't care what size they bought.

If the shirt didn't fit, they would cut it down the back.

And there were all the fashion changes. Most people don't realize it, but every year there are subtle changes made, even in ordinary shirts. The blue shirt from last year is usually a shade different from the shirt this year, as are all other colors. But blue is always the most popular color, year in and year out. The collars on shirts change. One year they are sort of short, next year they are a half an inch longer, and the next they might be a little bit longer than that. Then they'll go back to a short collar.

Calmer times: Nathan and Fred Block at ease at Wrightsville Beach Marina, about 1971

The same is true about the spread of a collar. Some years they are straight up and down, hardly room for a tie. And then they will gradually spread out so that the tie has plenty of room (which to me looks much better).

Then designers will put little sotskies on the shirt. Little messy things. Like the back loop, popular in the mid-1960s. It has no purpose except looks. And then customers will get a craze for exactly matched pockets. One and two pockets. Or then they go to two bias pockets.

The retailer remembers every pattern from the year before, and he will not buy last year's stuff unless you give him a big discount. Then there's the matter of a square tail or a long tail. Five buttons or six buttons. Top button showing, or a loop up at the top where it doesn't show.

All of a sudden about 1964, burgundy became the color for everything. We made burgundy shirts out of oxford broadcloth, or anything we could get in that color. For two years burgundy ruled the shirt world. And then when it went out of style, we had to close them all out for about half price.

Designers tried bottle green hoping for another burgundy, but it never worked. Another craze about that time was bleeding Indian madras. Why, I'll never know, because even though it looked good, you couldn't wash it with anything else because the color bled. And the fabric stank, and it came in short lengths, twenty to sixty yards long. Nothing matched. It was handmade.

Most cloth comes on rolls, anything from 100 to 200 yards, and it matches. But Indian madras was made in little workshops, not factories. What we'd do is lay it out in the warehouse and let it air out for two or three days before we used it. Then everybody got smart and used domestic madras that didn't bleed—and it matched.

Such are the trials and tribulations of the shirt manufacturer.

Watching the Pennies

Mitchell Allen started the Bank of North Carolina in Jacksonville, North Carolina, in 1952. Mitchell was very bright. He was a very good banker and knew how to do things. After he got it going pretty well, he opened a branch in Wallace, and then a branch in Wilmington.

In 1972, Mitchell's cousin Jere Freeman asked me to serve on the board of the Wilmington branch. I enjoyed my work with the bank. The stock was going up, and it presented a good opportunity. At the same time, differences of opinion had developed among Block family stockholders. John Burney, my attorney, called in Russell Robinson, a Charlotte attorney who worked with companies seeking to merge with other companies. At the time, we at Block were looking for that very thing. So I worked extensively with Russell for three months, and we planned some of the details for a merger.

A few months after the merger, Russell called one day and asked me if I'd like to go on the big board of the Bank of North Carolina. The bank's founder, Mitchell Allen, had died. As long as he was alive, the bank was going great guns, but after his death, everything was floundering. So Dick Spangler decided to come in and try to help. He had special feelings for the bank because his father, a major builder, had been one of the original incorporators. He brought on about half a dozen new directors. All of them except me were his old friends. He made his good friend Russell the new lawyer for the bank.

Members of the board, North Carolina National Bank. From left: Roddy Jones, James Worthington, Fred Block, Don Williamson, and Don Ahern. (Not pictured: C. D. Spangler, Albert Rachide, Meredith Senter, and Sidney Popkin.)

I got to know Dick for the first time when I rode with him and Russell to an organizational bank meeting in Jacksonville. I liked Dick a lot. He's a brilliant investor. I followed his stock picks more than once and was always happy that I did.

We all set a date for another meeting about thirty days after that. The bank was in bad condition because of deficient management. We were so poor that we got sandwiches sent in for lunch instead of going out to eat. We cut out any compensation to the directors, and we didn't pay the directors' expenses.

Dick Spangler really took over the bank and spent a lot of time working on what to do. After several false starts, he hired two men from New York to take charge of the day-to-day operations. That was the beginning of the recovery, and the bank went on to do great things after that.

The bank fired everyone who was expendable. The biggest factor that kept it going was that Dick and Russell went to Washington,

Cutting tables at the Block plant (Courtesy Lower Cape Fear Historical Society)

where banks always borrow short-term money from the Federal Reserve, and they negotiated a long-term loan that kept the bank from going bankrupt.

As things got better, we started eating lunch out again. We'd meet in the morning, go out to lunch, and sometimes meet again. The high point was the merger with NCNB, now the Bank of America. It was fun bringing a viable business back from near bankruptcy. Russell liked the way I was running Block and thought I would be an asset to the board. Once I got there, I became the watcher of the pennies.

You see, the shirt business is a business of pennies. If you watch the pennies, you make money. If you don't, you lose money. Anyone who has seen *The Pajama Game* on Broadway would understand more what I'm talking about. I saw it on Broadway several times. A workshop supervisor has to figure out how to meet union demands of a seven-and-a-half-cent raise per hour. It makes you think of every angle. You're always looking for better ways to do things. There's a lot of labor involved in making a shirt. And if you can find a better way that saves five cents a shirt, and you make a million shirts a year, that's a lot of money.

SPREADING OUT

As I said before, I was always pushing for increased production. We needed more shirts. We weren't producing enough in Wilmington to meet potential sales. I found out that they were making shirts in this little factory in Newport, North Carolina. One day I was up there and the man who owned the factory said he was interested in selling it and asked me if I would I be interested in buying it.

The man who opened that factory had worked for a woman named Mrs. Jackson who had a factory in Morehead City and he decided to open a factory in Newport, about seven or eight miles away. Mrs. Jackson was sort of a legend. She was very smart, very tough. I felt like he must be pretty good if he worked for her. He got a man in Newport to build a building and rent it to him, and he was smart enough to get machinery on credit from Singer Sewing Machine Company.

When he opened his little factory, they needed work. They made shirts for Campus, which kept a man down there all the time to check production. I found out they needed work, and I contracted with them to make shirts for us. And they were close enough so I could send my people up to have pretty good quality control. I kept a man or woman up there nearly all the time, to make sure our shirts were made well.

When your firm contracts with a company to produce shirts, you buy them and you send a representative into the factory to make sure they produce them like you want them produced. And you pay them so much a dozen. And then you sell them for profit. And it's a good deal because it just adds to your bottom line and you don't have to put up any bricks and mortar.

It worked for a while, and finally the man came to me one day and said, "I can't make shirts here anymore."

I said, "Why?"

And he said, "I don't have any money. I'm completely out of money and I'm going to have to close up."

So I said, "Can we buy your place?"

And he said, "Oh, that would be wonderful." So I talked to my father, stressing how much we needed more production. And he said, "Ah. We don't need another place. You can look at it if you want to, but I don't know what you want to buy a shirt factory for. We've got this factory. We've got one in Benson." Then he thought for a minute and said that if I could buy it and just take over the lease and machinery, it would be all right—to just go ahead and do it.

My father had to go to New York, so he left me in charge of handling the deal. I told our attorney, Ed Friedberg of Raleigh, what my father had said and what I wanted to do. He agreed to meet me in Newport the next morning to see what we could work out.

Up until this time, Ed had thought of me as a kid. He had worked with my father when I was just coming into the business. He never paid me that much attention. But when we met in Newport, he knew I wasn't a kid and that I knew what I was doing.

We talked to the people and we worked out what I considered a super, sure deal that would cost us almost no money at all. I asked if I should call my father. Ed told me, "No, you've made a very good deal here." So that was it.

Ed said, "Let's get an asset sale so they can't come back against us." If we hadn't done that, we'd have been in deep. The next day after we bought the business, the sheriff was right on our door and demanding

This trailer was one of three used to transport goods between Wilmington and Benson; the main factory usually sent cut shirts to Benson, which were sewn and returned to Wilmington as finished shirts.

that we pay off the notes owed by the previous owners.

I called Ed, who told me to show him the papers and let him know that I bought the assets and not the liabilities. So I did, and the sheriff said, "Sorry to have bothered you." Ed had protected us on all that sort of stuff.

If you buy a corporation, you buy all their problems. We didn't buy the corporation—just the assets. Any time I bought after that, I was very careful not to buy a corporation.

My father came back from New York and I said, "Guess what? We got a factory in Newport." Ed was there, too, and he said, "Nathan, he made a good deal. Don't say anything. Just go along with it. I was there and I guided him and everything worked out fine."

It did work out well. It was a super deal. And I was very proud of myself for engineering it. My father was the kind of person who was proud of me, but he never would say it. But I could tell he was proud of me doing that.

We finally got the Newport factory where it was producing at a very profitable rate. I doubled the size of it. I built onto the factory. It ended up making a higher quality shirt than we made in Wilmington.

One improvement that surprised me was something I learned in the Orient, where we employed a lot of transient workers. Normally, in Wilmington, I would never hire transient people. If a woman applied for a job and told me, "My husband is in the army—he's only going to be here six months," I wouldn't hire her, because it takes a long time to train people. It takes at least three months to teach someone how to operate the sewing machine. So I had a long-standing rule that I wouldn't hire servicemen's wives.

Bob George, my manager in Newport, got into a pinch one time and hired a transient worker, an Asian woman who mastered the job in two weeks. After that, I relaxed my rule. I found out in Newport that our Asian workers could learn in an average of three weeks. Whether it was due to a superior understanding of the work or a stronger determination to succeed, there was a notable difference. And that was a plus for that factory.

We had about fifty Japanese women working in Newport, and they had a wonderful work ethic. They chose to eat their lunch together, as a group. They would bring their own food and chopsticks from homes and chat in Japanese. They were a great asset to us because they worked hard. They didn't talk. And I learned that you could hire transient people if they were hard-working.

The man who owned the building was Mose Howard, who had a

Top right: Mildred Rackley, manager of the Benson plant, at her desk in the Wilmington office, 1966. Below: Bob George, manager of the Newport factory, stands at the cutting tables, 1966. (Courtesy Lower Cape Fear Historical Society)

filling station in Newport, on the way from New Bern to Morehead. He kept two buffaloes in his yard, and that enticed people to stop and buy gas. By the time I met him he had lots of money.

So everything was going well in Newport, but we still seemed to need more production. I was still in charge of production. I had a man named Winston who made some shirts for us and I looked at a factory in Garland, near Harrell's Store, but it didn't work out. Somebody else bought it out from under me, which was just as well.

We were looking for different sources, and one of our button suppliers was down here. Alton Ketchum was the button buyer, but I had to approve the purchases. Alton contracted for them and he was a good buyer. One day the button buyer came to me and said, "You know, I have a brother who lives in Rowland, where they've built a building that's sort of half finished and they're trying to get somebody to go in there as a manufacturer."

As it turned out, the button man's brother was on the city or county planning board. Six or eight of the board members had gotten together and put up money and built half the building. They were trying to entice people to come there. It hadn't attracted a tenant in six months, so they were getting pretty desperate. So I looked at the building and it looked good. I met with the people. They had a doctor there, and a druggist, and a Chevrolet dealer, and a farmer—the different people who were the mainstay of the town. And I met with them and told them everything looked pretty good and made them an offer.

Of course I had to go home and get everything approved by my own "board of directors," but I thought they would approve it: the board of directors was my father. I came home and I was thrilled because I got everything I wanted. So I even got the state to pay for the first thirty days' training for the different employees. I had heard of a government program, but it wasn't easy to get. Somebody in Rowland who had political connections, probably a lawyer, sort of carried the ball. I had to fill out a lot of papers and make a lot of statements.

They finished the building, and they owned a certain part of it and we owned a certain part. Everything worked out well. And I went down to South Carolina and located a woman named Mildred Rackley who used to work for my father and had opened the factory in Benson. Mildred really knew how to operate a factory. I persuaded her to come out of retirement and come to Rowland.

We had plenty of labor in Rowland, but the one problem was we had three different labor pools. We had whites, we had Native Americans, and we had blacks. They didn't mix. It was like, back in the old days, when the theaters in Wilmington or any other place in the South had a black entrance and a white entrance, and each group went in different places and used different water fountains. So when we went to Rowland, this man came up to me and said, "You know, you've got a problem. You've got three groups here. You've got the Indians. They won't go in the same bathroom as the blacks. And you've got the blacks and the whites. So you're going to have to have six bathrooms: three for the men and three for the women. And we did—until segregation was made illegal and we joined them back into two in accordance with OSHA's directions.

Rowland turned out to be a very good plant. The people were very efficient. We would send a truck up twice a week to Benson with parts of shirts. I used to take the station wagon full of collars and drive up and spend the night. The Native Americans were very loyal, good employees. And the blacks and whites were good, too, and mingled together. Later on, as we closed the different bathrooms, we had no problems. But it was a problem when we first went there.

By then we had a plant in Rowland, one in Benson, and one in Newport. And it was my job to go around, about every other week, to check on them. I was the big Pa for the plants. They looked up to me for what they needed and to tell me what was happening. They were all good plants and made very good money for us over that period of time, coming up to the year when we merged with National Service Industries.

In the early 1970s, it got to the point at Block where I was in the business, my brother David was in the business, and my cousin Franklin, and my cousin Howard. My father, my uncles, my Aunt Esther—they all had a legal say-so. And it got to a place where the business was important to different people for different things. My father was very good to Charlie. Each of them started out with a third of the stock. Joe and Esther shared the other third, with Joe holding twice as much as Esther. But my father kept accumulating, and he owned the most.

Of course, I wanted the business to grow. At the time, I was president. I was the one running the whole show at the time. My idea was to grow the business and to make it bigger and better, to keep on going. But then there were some in the family who cared more about getting dividends. They were older and they wanted money. And I can understand that. Everybody understood the positions of the others.

But it wasn't a harmonious place to work anymore. It's a miracle that the brothers got along so well, but when you mix up cousins and generations, it's tough. And we all got together and decided that the best thing would be to merge with another company so we could turn the stock into cash. Those who wanted to cash in, then, could do so. It took about a year to accomplish this.

National Service Industries in Atlanta seemed perfect for our situation. In August 1972, we merged with them, but it took two years for us to be able to sell our stock because we did not want to be tainted by the charge of an insider deal. That was all right because nobody cared about turning it into cash right away.

The deal worked. National was a good boss, in the beginning. They sponsored the opening of Block factories in Agua Prieta, Mexico, and Douglas, Arizona. Then we opened a factory in the Dominican Republic. We had contractors in Haiti. And National was very good at letting us branch out to do these kinds of things. And the company grew and grew and grew. It was close to a $100 million sales company, in 1985, when I stepped down.

When National bought us, they checked us for about six months to make sure everything was all right. They had to verify all our deeds and accounts to make sure everything was good. They sent a man around to our customers to ask if we were a good company and whether they would continue to do business with us.

In Mexico at that time, the government offered a special incentive plan: if you opened a plant in Mexico, you didn't have to pay taxes for five years. So that seemed like a very good deal to me. Wages were lower—sixty cents an hour there compared to about three dollars an hour here, so I wanted to go out there and take a look at it and see what they really had to offer. I went to Nogales first because we had cousins there. I had met them because they had been to Wilmington to visit about three years earlier. My grandfather had been out there to see them, so he knew them, but I didn't. Harvey Bracker's mother was my grandfather's first cousin. Harvey's father did very, very well there. He sent all his children to Mexico for their senior year in high school so they would really know how to speak Spanish and keep the business going well. The business was booming when I saw it, and it had been booming for years.

Ever the adoring mother, Sadie Block attends the opening of the North College Road factory in 1981 with Fred Block (left). In the background is Block salesman Abie Ruben, who with Henry Ormily co-owned Wilmington's upscale Plantation Club.

After National bought Block, they did a survey of what we needed and they decided we needed a vice-president of manufacturing. We had a big disagreement within the family about who it would be, and I decided to start looking for someone outside the company to fill the job. I called the Kurt Salmond engineering company to see if they knew of anybody. They knew a man who had recently had a heart attack, but who had recovered. I called the company he worked for to get a recommendation. The man's boss, Ben Raskind, took the call. I told him I was looking for someone and he said, "Well, I'm looking for a job too."

Ben was a big executive. I told him, "I don't know if I can pay what

EXPORT NUDGE—Armin H. Meyer (L), U.S. Ambassador to Japan, talks with Frederick Block of Wilmington president of Block Industries, about American made apparel during a U.S. trade mission to Japan. Nearby are an interpreter and Deputy Assistant Secretary of Commerce Stanley Nehmer. Twenty-four American businessmen traveled to Japan and Hong Kong to try to increase sales of American textiles and apparel in that area. The mission was sponsored by the American Apparel Manufacturers Association and the American Textile Manufacturers Institute.

BUSINESS ENCORE

Local businessman back from China

By Paul Jennewein
Business Editor

Frederick L. Block, president of Block Industries Division of National Services Industries Inc. in Wilmington, returned Friday after spending about 10 days in the People's Republic of China.

He was elated, reporting most of the business he'd set to accomplish had been accomplished.

"I had two purposes in mind," he said. "I wanted to buy ready-made shirts. And I wanted to set up a joint venture of manufacturing shirts in China."

Block said the joint venture might involve putting machinery in a Chinese plant or similar sort of operation. Negotiations were completed for a shipment of shirts to be sent in the late fall. Negotiations were started for a joint venture.

He said he was planning to return in May to discuss these plans further during the Canton Fair.

Doing business in China is different from business in other Oriental nation, Block indicated.

"I had been to Hong Kong, Tokyo, Korea and Taiwan many times before," he said. "This was the first time to the People's Republic of China."

His connection to China is a friend in Washington, D.C., a lawyer who was one of the first Americans to go over in 1972. Through this person, he obtained the needed invitation to visit Red China.

"You can only get in on an invitation," he explained. "Without a sponsor, you can't get a visa, you can't register at a hotel, travel or anything."

Visas or passes were only good for a particular city. He flew from Tokyo to Peking in five hours. His business was a textile firm took him to Canton.

"We had to go to the police station to get an exit visa to leave Canton."

Business is conducted primarily with a trade group, or corporations, of which there are 15 in China. They deal in different types of commodities. He had to start with the corporation at National Textile Corp. The headquarters for each were 10 groups in Peking.

Within each corporation, there are groups of autonomous organizations which are fiercely competitive with each other. The Canton group was the one with which Block did business.

All the people with whom I dealt spoke English," he said. "They were good negotiators, and liked it.

The quality of products in China was superior to any in the Far East."

Such oral negotiations took longer than they would in the United States. Many of the Chinese business liked to think about the various offers and ideas during negotiations.

"That would have taken about three days here, took us till then," he said.

Block indicated he was impressed with the attitude of Chinese.

"They have a strong, good feeling for Americans. It's a welcome change from some of the other countries where attitude is different."

A workweek is six days for the average Chinese factory worker — eight hours a day for 48 hours in the week. The take-home pay of the worker is about $36 a month.

"Most of them seem happy and well content," he said. "I personally think they'll be a dominant force in the Far East."

Frederick L. Block of Wilmington, president of Block Industries Division of National Services Industries Inc., displays a miniature Chinese dragon boat made of rice straw that he brought back from the People's Republic of China. Block was in China to order shirts and set up a joint venture textile plant in Red China.

Above: Trade delegation departs for China, 1970s (Wilmington Star-News). Left: The Star-News reports Fred Block's return from an overseas business trip, March 25, 1979.

you want to get." He thought for a minute and said, "I think we can work it out."

He came down to Wilmington the very next day. I liked him a lot and hired him. He made a great v.p. of manufacturing. We worked together for years.

In 1973, I went out West because I had been thinking about building another factory, but I also wanted to meet my cousins and see their business. Their store in Nogales, Arizona, was right across the border from Nogales, Mexico. And it was an interesting situation in Nogales,

Trade mission attorney Martin Klingenberg and Fred Block at the Great Wall of China, 1979 (photo by Paul Jennewein)

because Mexico had a very high system of tariffs, so the well-to-do people in Mexico came across the border to Nogales, among other cities, to buy most of their clothes and things. So in a little town like Nogales they had about twenty stores that catered to the Mexicans. If somebody got married, they'd come across the border and buy a few thousand dollars' worth of stuff for a trousseau.

I looked around Nogales and it was fine. But then I went over to Douglas and they had, for some reason, a lower wage scale than Nogales and had more labor available. So it seemed the right thing to do. But I was out there with a man from National and one night in a bar, he and I sat down and wrote down the plusses and minuses of each city. The only plus for Nogales was that Harvey was there.

The next day we went to see a lawyer in Douglas and got the wheels turning to open a factory in Douglas. And about six months later, after buying land for a factory in Douglas and land in a sister city that was bigger than Douglas—Agua Prieta—we had a temporary factory in both cities. So we started operating in about June of 1974. We had to cut shirts in Douglas and send them over to Agua Prieta to be made, then send them back to Douglas to be pressed. And then we trucked them back to Wilmington to be integrated into our other shirts. It was a very profitable operation.

We made jackets in Mexico, too—leather jackets. We made the lightweight jackets in the regular factories because they were similar in manufacture to shirts. The heavyweight jackets were made in Korea.

The builder for the Douglas building was from Tucson. He was a sharp builder. He had done well and liked to pilot his own plane. He was getting ready to develop some property he owned in Baja California, on the western Pacific coast of Mexico. He was going to develop there because land was cheap and building was cheap, and it would be a wonderful getaway for anyone who lived Arizona, California, or Nevada. He was trying to sell me a group of several lots as an investment. I was supposed to meet him and fly down with him to Baja, because they had no plane service at that time. But before we scheduled the visit he was killed in a plane crash. I felt very sad and scared.

NEW YAWK

One place I always felt good and usually felt very comfortable was in New York City. My father opened the New York office soon after World War II. He started with one room in the Empire State Building, probably 1,500 square feet. Bernie Steinmetz was the shirt salesman for the New York office, and he continued to work there for many years. And we kept growing from there. By the time I left the company in 1985, we occupied a whole floor, the 26th; before that, we had the 44th floor.

New York was primarily the sales and buying location for the company. In fact, we had numerous companies that operated out of New York. I was in New York at least one week of every month from 1975 until 1985. Before that I was there at least a week every two or three months. I was there to check on things, but my primary job was to aid the salesmen in selling the product—and negotiate large contracts for cloth and finished shirts in the Far East. Also, when I was in New York, I set up meetings in the Orient, to finalize purchase of the shirts we bought to resell. It had to be done in New York because the people in the Orient worked through New York. Every day in that office, there were long telexes of communications with the Orient.

David had been working in New York since about 1959. He went up there as Joe's assistant, but he worked his way up until he was the sales manager and piece goods buyer in that office. We worked well together, and there were always things we needed to catch up on.

When I wasn't working, I just enjoyed hanging out in the city. My last apartment there was at 240 Central Park South, seventeenth floor. It overlooked the park—and I spent many hours sitting in the park, just people watching. For some reason people often asked me directions in New York. Some asked me where they should eat—and occasionally people in the

restaurants there would ask me what they should order. I guess they took me for a New Yorker—until I answered with a Southern accent.

On Sundays I usually visited Chinatown. I had some favorite things I used to like to do in Chinatown. One was to go to a dim sum restaurant and eat more than usual. Another was to visit a place where the fish swam in the tanks and you could point to the one you wanted for dinner that night. They would take your fish to the kitchen and cook it. Talk about fresh seafood—that was it. Chinatown in New York was so much like China itself, I had a hard time deciding which was which sometimes.

Back in the city, I also had my favorite haunts. For lunch, I liked to go to the delis. The Carnegie was my favorite. For several months, there was a 9:00 p.m. nonstop flight to Wilmington. I had time to stop by the Carnegie on the way to the airport and get a pastrami on rye, with tomato pickles and cucumber pickles, for the trip home. The flight just took one hour. By the time we got to Wilmington, the plane smelled just like the Carnegie. I also brought sushi onto the plane many times.

For dinner in New York, I liked Shunlee, Gabriel's, the Saloon, the

Palm, a little Italian spot called the Grotto, and a kosher restaurant, the Kasbah, I think. I loved them all—and numerous other ones that opened and closed.

But it wasn't just the business or the food or the park. I just *love* New York. It's my second home. When Frank Sinatra came out with "New York, New York," it seemed almost like an anthem to me. I remember dancing to that song in 1997. I was giving the party, and the band director knew how much I loved the song. He strung out the music so that it went on and on. It was the last song of the evening. And I just kept dancing.

Longtime Block employees Joe Maultsby (left; also see photo, page 109), and Alton Ketchum (right), with Nathan Block at the new factory, about 1981.

TODAY

I loved my work at Block Industries but there was a lot of stress in the mid-1980s, and there were also a few misunderstandings. I resigned from the firm in 1985.

Om January 1990, I had the chance to visit the house in Forest Hills where my family had lived for so long. Back when I was young I'd saved a few Indian head pennies, which I hid over the door facing in my bedroom but then forgot by the time my father put the house on the market. I remembered, all these years later, to check. But they were gone.

Today, wherever I go in Wilmington I see a different place. My first neighborhood seemed contemporary way back when—and now it's in the Historic Overlay. That really makes you feel old.

I ride by our old house on Chestnut Street and I wonder who lives there. I wonder if they would have any interest in knowing my father once kept liquor hidden under the steps.

I've lost many of the good friends I had back then. Weddell Harriss died years ago in New York, when he fell from an apartment window. I don't think he ever got over the death of his little brother, Thomas. He was never the same after that—he became quiet and withdrawn. And Louis Hanson died, too. I think about them often.

Time brings some surprises. I remember the Wrights' fine house at 15th and Chestnut Streets: as I child, I would peek through the shrubs to see their private garden. A few years ago, Eleanor Wright Beane became a friend I felt close to. After a span of nearly seventy years, I finally got to know her.

When I see the house at 711 Forest Hills Drive, I don't have quite as much emotion. My life wasn't as contained there as it was on Chestnut Street because I was older. I could get away more. I think about the day in 1969 when my father decided to sell the Forest Hills house because he was afraid my mother was working herself to death in the garden. I also think about my parents entertaining with their little parties in the basement.

Most of my parents' close friends, like the Steins and Bill Zimmer, are gone now. But Roberta Zimmer and her children are thriving. I remember when the Zimmer family moved to Wilmington. They were just getting started, and Ma Sadie took them under her wing. She even helped nurse one of the children through an illness. They've done well, and the boys—Herbert, Jeffrey, and Allen—are now big businessmen. Some of the Zimmers along with Hyman Brody, the Stadiems' good friend, have been developing the Mayfaire Town Center in Wilmington, a planned community as big as some whole towns. And now there is a whole wing of the hospital named for the Zimmers.

I think about my mother's devotion to me. She was a mother consumed with love for her children. I think about my father, and wish I had asked him many things. His early life in Baltimore, where he was segregated by religion, stayed with him. He grew up in a Jewish neighborhood. My upbringing was very different from his.

But it is William Block, my grandfather, whom I would like to question most of all. "Tell me about your family in Riga. How did it feel to leave your mother and your homeland when you were so young? What were you thinking when your face shone in the synagogue?" Still, I think I know the answer to that. There was something going on there that cannot be put into words.

The Temple of Israel seems much more beautiful now than it did when I was a boy. And I am glad that the synagogue contains a room dedicated to my grandfather. My father was on the building committee of the synagogue, and he helped sway them to cut costs—among other influences I'm guessing he had.

But when I ride down the 300 block of Walnut Street I am very sad that the old synagogue is gone. I have many warm feelings that go back to that place and to the sweet love my grandfather showed me there. If I could draw, I would draw a picture of those old men up there on the bema—those happy faces.

I don't know what my grandfather would think of me going to St. James Church on occasion. Of course I could blame it on Ma Sadie for sending me there to kindergarten.

As for the old Block facto-ry, I ride by and wish it was still red brick. A new owner has bought it and painted it yellow. When I see the building, it's the odd things that stand out in my mind—like the day we caught a girl stealing shirts. The back seat of her car was full of new shirts. I said, "What are you doing stealing our shirts?!" And she said, "Don't you know? A lot of people who work here steal your shirts!"

Greenfield Street wing of Block Shirts

What would I do different at work? I regret one of the firings.

Still, I am proud that we gave jobs to so many hard-working people. I'm proud every time someone walks up to me and says they used to work for Block. And I'm proud of the products. We made good shirts that were affordable. Millions and millions of them. Shirts are not lasting things, like buildings or monuments. But we filled a need and provided employment in the process.

Retirement has given me time to learn things I didn't have time for when I worked. Well, maybe I *did* have the time. But when I was away from the factory, I looked for recreation as hard as I looked for profit at work.

Now, though, I have time to read and learn things I wasn't even aware I didn't know. The kind of business I was in drank up time and didn't lend itself to other kinds of learning. If I had it to do all over again, I would read more. And I might have joined a civic club. My father didn't think there was a place in the shirt world for Rotary or Civitans or Kiwanis because our

Block factory workers, above: Magdalene Johnson (left), supervisor of the pressers, and Doris Ashe in the pressing department, about 1984. Below, from left: Switchboard operator Holly Long, printing department supervisor Brad Murray, and pressing department supervisor Magdalene Johnson, about 1985.

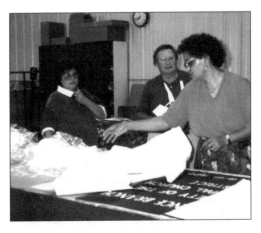

customer base wasn't in Wilmington. But I'm not sure he was right.

For these past few years, I have had many happy times and lots of laughter. Those are two different things, but it's very good when they

Caught in thought: Fred Block at Figure Eight Island, about 1992
(photo by Susan Block)

go together. I have seen a lot of coincidences that I guess just might be somebody upstairs looking after me.

But my most serious thought these past few years is about purpose. I watch and see wasted talents and money thrown to the wind and it makes me sad and sometimes it makes me angry. Trifling is what I call it. I don't like trifling and I never have. But it hasn't been until recently that I thought of it in a religious way, or that I saw what I consider to be a good work ethic as stewardship.

I'm seventy-seven now. Age makes you less earthbound.

I think God has some serious plan for each of us to produce and to work hard at something special, and if that is what we are supposed to do we will have some uncanny knack for it. But we will still have to work at it, every single day. Or, as my grandfather would say, six days a week.

I just thank God that I was made to be a shirtmaker, and that is exactly what I did and what I wanted to do. Our company put food on many tables, put clothing on countless backs, and gave jobs to hundreds of people who had been turned away by others.

I've been very fortunate.

––––––

NOTES

1. The name of William Block's mother is variously listed in sources as Rebecca and as Rachel. A newspaper article gives Rachel, while William's death certificate, and another family document, say Rebecca.

   Precise records do not survive, but William is believed to be the youngest of the siblings.
2. Undated obituary, *Charlotte (N.C.) Observer.*
3. *Wilmington Morning Star,* March 29, 1925.
4. *Wilmington Morning Star,* March 4, 1923. Block Manufacturing Co., Inc. records, Special Collections, University of North Carolina at Wilmington.
5. Undated article from Kinston newspaper.
6. It may be of interest that William Block and Lena Wolk Block once sailed to Riga to see William's mother, who gave him the ring his father had given to her.
7. *Wall Street Journal,* July 5, 1992; *Wilmington Star-News,* July 10, 1992.

This book was composed in the Adobe Garamond, Copperplate Gothic, and Ribbon typefaces in Quark XPress 4.1 for the Macintosh computer.

Of making many books there is no end.
ECCLESIASTES 12:12

Winoca Press